DECIDE

*How to Make the Right Decision
Every Time and in Every Circumstance
No Matter What*

by Robert RJ Regan

Copyright © 2020 by Robert RJ Regan
All rights reserved. This book or any portion thereof
may not be reproduced or used in any manner whatso
everwithout the express written permission of the publisher
except for the use of brief quotations in a book review.

Printed in the United States of America

First Printing, 2020

ISBN 978-1-7349568-0-1

Forest City Publications
1658 Milwaukee Ave # 100-16118
Chicago, IL 60647
(815) 708-6474

www.forestcitypublications.com

Contents

Preface..1

You Are Here...5

One Bad Decision..9

How to Begin with the End in Mind.......................17

Decide to Decide..23

Why Is It Sometimes So Hard to Decide?.............41

Know The Recipe for Dumb
Decision-Making (So You Can Avoid It).............47

The Relationship between Decision-Making,
Control, and Anxiety...59

The Recipe For Wise Decision-Making
(So You Can Be the Author of Your Life).............67

Choose Your Health..79

Choose Who You Are
and Who You Hang With......................................91

How to Choose Freely...109

Make a Choice and Check the Results...............123

Tools For Decision Making.................................155

The End is the Beginning....................................167

Preface

Although this book was 50 years in the making, it was actually written in record time as the result of a challenge between Tony Rubleski, CEO and President of MindCapture Group, and me. You see, Tony and I were meeting, like we routinely do, to go over goals, business ideas and to provide mutual encouragement when he shared a book idea with me.

"Well, write it!" I said.

Everyone is busy, but we always find the time to do the things that are important. The decision needed to be made to just do it. So I challenged him by saying, "I bet I can finish my next book before you do."

And the race was on!

We set a 30 day goal to complete our projects. We held weekly teleconferences for accountability and pushed the goal back a couple of weeks during the Christmas break.

The result in less than two months was two new completed manuscripts!

Everything changes when a decision is made. The decision to make a call, start (and finish) a project, or the decision NOT to do something. You must decide. But how, who and what to decide can be daunting with our ever increasing access to information.

This book was written to help in the decision making process. If you are looking for help to make a decision, get unstuck or continue on a path, then this book is for you.

Our life consists of the decisions we choose to make or not to make.

Buying this book may turn out to be the best decision of your life.

Introduction
You Are Here

You are one decision away from a totally different life.

Yet many of us fail to decide, or we do so too late to have that big impact we wanted to have.

What holds us back?

We don't want to look foolish or to be wrong. We want to make the right decision, and we're not guaranteed to know that the one we're making is the right one.

This is a short yet powerful book to help you with that.

It's a look at the psychological impact of decision-making and the strategies to not only make the best decision but to make those decisions the right ones.

It's time to decide!

The best decision you will ever make is when you make the decision to make your own decisions.

Buying this book will be the best decision you ever make.

And it all begins with the decision to decide.

Fish or cut bait.
Poop or get off the pot.
Get busy living or get busy dying.

Decide to be intentional.

Ready, shoot, aim.

"Perfection and productivity are mutually exclusive."
David Allen

In other words, if you are waiting for it to be right before you move, you'll never move, and it will never be right.

Productivity, action and engagement is what makes perfection possible.

The first question toward understanding your power to decide is to answer this question.

Do you create or do you tolerate? God created us in His image, so we are creators. Whatever you allow or "tolerate," you put your stamp of approval on it. One reason that I hate the word tolerant. You only tolerate what is bad. You enjoy what is good.

What you allow, you approve. What you have, you tolerate. What you allow you approve, what you measure gets accomplished and what you reward you get more of.

"We are destroying speculations and every lofty thing raised up against the knowledge of God, and we are taking every thought captive to the obedience of Christ." 2 Corinthians 10:15 NASB

"Taking thoughts captive means controlling them instead of letting them control you." — Priscilla Shirer

In the movie *Scent of a Woman*, Colonial Slade knew the

right path but didn't take it. Why? Because it was too damn hard. It is hard, but like all things worth having, the hard work is worth it.

"If you view yourself as a victim you become your own oppressor." Candace Owens

Your best life starts with your decision to decide.

And it starts on the next page.

Chapter One

One Bad Decision

In the movie *Indiana Jones and The Last Crusade*, Indiana Jones had just completed all of the death defying challenges to get to the Holy Grail. Then, in typical Steven Spielberg fashion, a curve ball is thrown and at the last moment, Indy's nemesis Walter Donovan shows up, gun brandished and ready to steal the prize from Indy.

Mr. Donovan must choose among the dozens of cups and is at a loss for which one to choose. He relies on the expert, Dr. Elsa Schneider, to choose for him, who intentionally gives him the wrong cup and when he drinks, his life is mysteriously and aggressively taken from him.

At which point the old frail knight, who was guarding the Holy Grail dryly said, "He chose poorly."

But the biggest risk of all is not making a decision and allowing others to make your decisions for you.

Yes, one bad decision can change your life forever. Most of the decisions we make each day don't appear that important. But the biggest risk of all is not making a decision and allowing others to make your decisions for you.

Making a good decision can have a very profound and

positive effect on your life, just like a bad decision can. Cemeteries and prisons are filled with men who made the wrong decision. One decision can change your life, for better or for worse.

Henry David Thoreau in Walden wrote, "I went to the woods because I wished to live deliberately, to front only the essential facts of life, and see if I could not learn what it had to teach, and not, when I came to die, discover that I had not lived."

Think of it in terms of shopping. Have you ever paid too much for something? The late-night TV impulse purchase, the luxurious timeshare or automobile? What about that big "dream house" that turned into a nightmare?

Or maybe, you missed out on a great deal, an investment opportunity, or asking someone out on a date?

Or possibly, your 30, 40, 50 or 60 years old and ask, "Where did my life go?"

It can be a sickening feeling when you consider what you did or did not do, especially when you fell for someone else's plan for your life.

There is an old parable of a little bird and a wise owl. The little bird was crying, covering his eye with his little wing when the owl looked down and asked, "What's the matter little bird?" The little bird pulled his wing away showing his missing eye. The owl exclaimed, "Oh, I see, you're crying because the bigger bird plucked out your eye!" To which the little bird replied, "No, I'm crying because I let him."

Generally speaking, it is not the one-time catastrophic events that cause the greatest harm. Like the little bird losing his eye. No, instead it is the seemingly innocent decisions, or lack of decision that has no immediate effect, but has a massive long-term impact.

This idea is beautifully illustrated in the poem, "The Night They Burned Shanghai," by Robert D. Abrahams, written in 1938. The poem ends with these telling words:

> "For some men die by shrapnel,
> And some go down in flames,
> But most men perish inch by inch,
> In play at little games."

These "little games" are like termites to your house, or the little pleasures you spend your time and money on that add no real lasting value to your life. Think of the 4 hours of streaming shows, and social media every day, to go along with the $300 cable bill, $600 auto lease and $500 in meals eaten out each month. Those things seem innocent enough, but repeated over 10 years? That's quite a cost!

This book is all about decisions. In it you will learn the anatomy of decision making; why it can be so hard to make them, why we get sucked into bad ones, and why we fail to act on good ones.

Count the Cost and Be Intentional

Like Mr. Thoreau's words on living a deliberate life, Stephen Covey, in his best-selling book *Seven Habits of Highly Effective People*, talks about **beginning with the end in mind**. Even Moses in the *Bible* asks God in Psalm 90:12 ". . . teach us to number our days, That, we may present to You a heart of wisdom."

The apostle Paul also writes of the importance of being

decisive. In his letter to the Ephesians, he writes, "Therefore be careful how you walk, not as unwise men but as wise, making the most of your time, because the days are evil. So then do not be foolish but understand what the will of the Lord is." Ephesians 5:15-17 NASB

Why reference, the *Bible*? In Hebrews 4:12 tells us that the *Bible* is alive and active. Meaning that the words in it are just as true today as they were when they were written thousands of years ago.

70 Conscious Decisions Each Day

What is a decision and what exactly does it mean to decide?

Consider these great men and what they said about deciding.

"Whether you think you can or think you can't, you're right." — Henry Ford

"We are shaped by our thoughts; we become what we think." — Buddha

"Believe you can and you're halfway there." — Teddy Roosevelt

"The happiness of your life depends on the quality of your thoughts." — Marcus Aurelius

"Our thoughts make us what we are." — Dale Carnegie

But, if you don't know where you are going, it really doesn't matter what you choose, until it's too late, of course, when all of the options are gone. I'm reminded of the *Alice In Wonderland* exchange below:

One day Alice came to a fork in the road and saw a Cheshire cat in a tree. "Which road do I take?" she asked. "Where do you want to go?" was his response. "I don't know," Alice answered. "Then," said the cat, "it doesn't matter."

And, as David Allen says, "every road will bug you."

Without a goal or a purpose for your life, decisions will be fuzzy at best and irrelevant at worst. A goal will instantly crystalize your thinking and immediately simplify your decision-making process. Why? Because when you have a goal, by definition you are eliminating choices that do not align with your goal. On the other hand; if you don't have a goal or know what you want, you're probably already thinking, "How do I choose my goal and decide on my purpose?"

The first step is to just decide and then see what happens. Then you can decide to make course corrections along the way as you get more and more feedback from the consequences of your choice.

But you might say, I can't decide!

The first step is to just decide and then see what happens.

The Nicholas Sparks movie *The Choice* opens with this monologue:

"Now, pay attention, 'cause I'm about to tell you the secret to life.

You ready?

The whole damn thing is about decisions, time, seemingly insignificant decisions that clear the road for monster truck life-altering ones.

You see, every path you take leads to another choice, and some choices can change everything.

Every damn moment of the rest of your life hangs on them.

And, boy, do I have a choice I have to make."

I get it. Decision-making can be intimidating. It makes sense to stop for a minute, and actually look at the word "decide," and what it means. And the best way to understand what it means is to look at how decision-making is best practiced.

Remember, you are your choices. Every choice affects every other choice, and every choice has consequences. For example, if you choose not to save, you've chosen to be broke. If you choose not to work out and eat right, you've chosen to be sick.

Chapter Two

How to Begin with the End in Mind

This is how you begin with the end in mind - it begins with imagination. Thinking like this will start the process of crystalizing your decision-making.

Imagination is a good place to start the goal-setting process. Imagine what you want your life to be like. Be honest about what you really want, not what somebody else says you want. How healthy do you want to be? How happy? How wealthy? How many friends?

Start writing things down. What do you want to be, do and have? Is it things, like how you will live your life, the type of person to marry, and who will be around you when you die. Medium-size issues are those like where you want to live, how much and where you want to travel, and what type of career to have. Then there are little things like toys to buy, skills to develop, and things to see.

I have a goal list of over 100 things. Some of them are short term goals, some are longer term. Some are goals that I am currently working on and others are in a holding pattern until later. The point is to have a list and refer to it often.

Imagination is important, so you can pull from the future benefit of what you want to help motivate you in the present time. When you really feel it by using your imagination, you can literally trick your mind into thinking it has already happened. For example, imagine what it is like to visit the beach in Mexico. You just completed a major project at work. The calendar has been marked off with "X's" as you counted down the days. Had a diet and workout plan, because you knew you would be on the beach. Your book has been picked out to read.

Then you close your eyes and imagine what the surf sounds like crashing onto the sand. The roar and crash, then the slow retreat where you hear little bubble sounds as the water filters through the sand as the wave retreats to the sea. Then off in the distance, you hear a seagull chirp, as the soft Mexican music of a mariachi band is playing at the hotel.

The smell of saltwater mixes with the aroma of fresh corn tortillas, guacamole and a margarita that was just placed next to your hammock that is strung between two palm trees as you swing ever so slightly in the soft breeze.

The power of imagination is found in how it impacts your behavior now. You'll have an easier time sticking to your plan because of the decision you made, and the way you use your imagination to experience that beautiful beach here and now. You'll be far more likely to ensure you get the time off and the funds saved to visit that beach, too, because you had a definite goal.

Use Your Imagination to Begin at the Very End - The End of Life

If you want to get really serious about it, begin at the very end - the end of your life. That is the ultimate decision. What will the end of your life look like? You do get to decide this. I was *fortunate* enough to have that forced upon me at the age of 23 when I was taken hostage at gunpoint while working at a bank in Indianapolis. There is nothing like having a man stick a gun in your face and say he is going to shoot you to help crystallize your thinking!

What if I died? Was I living the life I wanted to?

In the *Lord of the Ring*s trilogy, there was a crystal ball that allowed the person to see what was going on in other parts of the realm. Although, we do not have a crystal ball, we do have something equivalent. We have our imagination and other people.

My experience of being held at gunpoint forced me to consider the end and what I wanted out of life. Not everyone has a crystallizing experience thrust upon them like this, but it is truly important for everyone to consider. In South Korea, they take this very seriously. They have a ritual where you are actually placed into a coffin and a funeral message is given to illustrate the temporary nature of our lives so that you will live more intentionally.

I had a *Bible* study leader hand out actual mortuary toe tags with my name on it to illustrate the same point. You too can ask yourself what you want your life to look like when you draw your final breath. Who will be around you when you die? What will they say about you? What will God say? You get the idea.

At this point in time, you may not be sure what you want and that's okay. I didn't for a long time and still, to this day, I still refine my thinking, desires and goals. Mostly that is done through paying attention, listening to other people, and being open to what the world has to offer. This is part of the process of decision-making. It is what I was talking about when I said, "You make a decision and move forward, adjusting as you see the effects of that decision. We're really never done deciding, observing, and refining. It's a lifelong process."

That doesn't take into account the curveballs in life either! I wanted to be a husband and father. Never in a million years would I have thought I would be divorced. Yet, 21 years later, here I am, a divorced man. Circumstances change, and as they do your goals sometimes have to shift, too, as you reevaluate and adjust.

When I was married, we got invited to a lot of fundraisers. I mean a LOT of them! After a while, I got a little worn out by the whole ordeal, but I knew this was important to my wife and thus was a part of my life. I decided to go, after all. It was my choice to place my wife's desire over my comfort. At the same time, I want to enjoy my life. So, I decided that I had better find a way to enjoy the events we were destined to be going to for years to come. As a result, I started to pay closer attention to these events.

At one party and then another I noticed that the oldest people in the room were almost always sitting in the corner. Alone. An idea was hatched!

I started going to these events with a new purpose. We would show up to the party where I would make the rounds and customary introductions. Then my focus would shift to find the golden gem at the party. I would order a glass of wine and go over to the seasoned citizen where I would introduce myself, tell them a little bit about me, and simply ask, "If you were my age all over again, what advice would you give to yourself?" Then I would shut up and listen.

Old people are great. They have a ton of experience and wisdom, along with a filter-free story-telling ability. They are not politically correct, they are not trying to impress anybody, they just speak their truth, and tell the stories of their life. It was awesome! I learned so much about life, people, and what is important while we are here on earth.

One of the biggest regrets I heard over and over wasn't the mistakes they made, but the risks they didn't take. Another big one was spending too much time at the office, or on their business, and missing out on family events and children growing up. Taking care of their physical body. Oh, and their teeth was another big one. Take care of your teeth!

Take some time to ponder your life, what you want, and then interact with people that have been in your shoes. They are everywhere and they love to talk!

If you want a specific tool to help uncover your purpose and goals for your life, I recommend the *Self Authoring Tool* created by Jordan Peterson. It is an online program that will help you discover what makes you tick and put together a plan for getting there.

Chapter Three

Decide to Decide

You may be thinking, "Why should I decide? Why not let somebody else decide and take the risk?"

There is an element of truth in that, but you also need to remember that by allowing someone else to decide for you, you made the decision to do that. You made a decision!

When you were younger you had parents, teachers and others who helped guide your development. As you mature, you should be the one making decisions. Everyone is different, and has different experiences, but principles reign supreme. Mature people take control and make decisions. Immature people are out of control and make excuses. Maturity isn't an age either, maturity is a mindset.

I know many 50-year-old teenagers. Give them a chance to be 21 again and they would be right back on the beach in Daytona for spring break. I also know teenagers that are thinking and acting like 50-year-olds. I was friends with one in middle school and high school. His name is Scott Stearns.

My best friend Scott Stearns used to wear a suit to school and carry a briefcase and the *Wall Street Journal* everywhere he went. This dude was like the Michael J. Fox character in the 1980's sitcom *Family Ties*. Scott didn't care that others were making different decisions about what they wore and what they cared about. He had a plan, and he was deciding every day to act in accordance with that plan.

Even a blind man could see it was only a matter of time before Scott moved to the east coast and was working in New York City.

What is the point? Immature people let others make decisions for them. Mature people take control and make their own decisions. That doesn't mean they don't take advice or get input from others, but they stop acting like children and take control.

Janet Jackson, in her song "Control," starts with the following lyrics:

When I was 17, I did what people told me.
Did what my father said,
and let my mother mold me.
But that was long ago.
I'm in Control - Never gonna stop!
Control - To get what I want.
Control - I like to have a lot.
Control - Now I'm all grown up.

So how do you know you're making your own decisions? The tricky part is that there isn't just one way to make decisions. We are all individuals, and what works for you may not work for me. But there are elements that every good decision-making method shares. I've put together principles of decision-making that applies to everyone. These are the basics you need to lay a foundation and create a framework. For each principle, I've included examples of decision-making tricks and tips.

By the way, in case you haven't figured it out yet, the second most important decision you will ever make is to start making your own decisions and take 100% control and ownership of your life. The most important decision was the one you made to purchase this book!

Principle #1: Being Unclear is Being Unkind

The first principle is that you must be clear. Being clear is far more important than most people realize. Not only is not being clear about what you want confusing, it is unkind. Lacking clarity makes things complicated, and then you can't confidently move forward, because you will always be second guessing yourself. And if you happen to be in a leadership position, that is quite frankly, just unkind. Make the decision, make it right, and move forward. If you really do need to change, then confidently move forward in that direction. Do not be timid.

Why is decision-making important?

Why are decision-making skills important? Decision-making skills have always been one of the traits that appeal the most to employers. The reason it has been given so much importance is that the ability of making a decision, as well as sticking to it, is considered to be the cornerstone of any good leadership.

Webster defines decision as the act or process of deciding. To decide is to make a final choice or judgment. Looking at the root words from decide, we see it is from Latin descent. It's "cide." "Cide" originates from the Latin word *caedere* meaning "to kill."

Here are some other words that have the same root:

Homicide - to kill a person
Suicide - to kill oneself

Genocide - to kill a group of people
Pesticide - to kill insects
Fungicide - to kill fungus

There are more, but the point is they all mean to cut off or kill something. So, when we decide, what are we killing? We are killing off all of the other choices, and when we do that, we limit our options.

When you decided to marry your spouse, you eliminated all the other options. When you decided to have children, you killed off the option to not have children.

Knowing this is helpful because it starts to illuminate why making decisions can be so difficult. There is finality to decision-making, and we like to have options. Not deciding something gives us flexibility and apparent freedom. But, when you fail to make a decision, you are actually stuck. Yes, your options remain available, but you also can't go anywhere. But never lose sight of the fact that time keeps on tickin' and some decisions are only available for a short time. Once the time has past, they are gone forever. Here's an example for you: you can't wait too long to have a child or the opportunity passes you by.

The other reason it is hard to make decisions is because once you decide something, you are committing yourself to doing it, and if you don't, it will cause you mental anguish. Even the *Bible* mentions this in James 4:17: "Therefore, to one who knows the right thing to do and does not do it, to him it is sin."

James is saying that once you decide the right thing to do, if you don't do it, you will be living in your own little personal hell that you created with inaction.

There is something that is harder on you that can be even more difficult than making a decision, or even a bad decision, and that's to not make a decision. By letting things slide, and being wishy washy through life, you are missing out on what life has to offer. You are limiting your own potential and shortchanging yourself and those you love.

In Proverbs 13:12, Solomon wrote, "Hope deferred makes the heart sick." By deferring your hope through indecision and inactivity, you are actually creating a state of depression and anxiety within you. It will eat away at your soul.

This spirit of being timid is not honorable or "god-like" in the slightest. In fact, the *Bible* specifically mentions this in 2 Timothy 1:7: "For God has not given us a spirit of timidity, but of power and love and discipline."

If you are being timid, understand that this is not a spirit from God. We are created to make choices, to use our good judgment to decide, and then to act in accordance with those decisions.

To help eliminate timidity, there are simple and bold things that you can do. By doing so, you will eliminate procrastination, increase accountability, and even motivate yourself to get busy.

One of the best examples of this traces back to 1519 with one of history's most inspiring leadership stories. Hernán Cortés led a large expedition consisting of 600 Spaniards, 16 or so horses, and 11 boats to Mexico. The goal: capture a magnificent treasure. Once Cortés made landfall, he ordered the ships be destroyed by burning them. This sent a clear and definite message to his men: there is no turning back. They either win or they die.

You may consider this the biggest "Wait, What?" moment in history! Imagine if you were one of his soldiers. What are you thinking, you crazy captain?!?! But, with no exit strategy and no other option, burning the ships had the proper and intended outcome: intense focus and motivation to win! Within two years, he succeeded in his conquest of the Aztec empire.

When you make a decision, you are eliminating options and in essence "burning your ships." Eliminating the decision of sailing home unless they won the battle. Going "all in" has a similar effect. We see this on the World Series of Poker. Once a guy gets to the point where he pushes all of his chips into the center of the table, he typically stands up, intensely focused on what will happen next. He either wins, or he goes home.

My friend Bobby has a fitness business that focuses on targeted and specific strength training. He told me his story of an eight-week period where he had to change locations due to a rent/landlord issue. During that 8 week period, he was concerned that he might lose clients and possibly his business along with it, so he started interviewing for other fitness jobs at larger more established fitness centers in town, just to "cover his bases." Upon hearing this, his brother pulled him aside and said, "No way buddy. You're all in. You give yourself an escape route and you'll be tempted to take it."

I will talk more about making decisions "stick" later in the book, but for now, understanding some ways to eliminate your tendency to put things off, or stay accountable can help eliminate one of the fears of decision-making. That fear is the fear of failure. Once you effectively motivate yourself by burning your ships, you massively stack the odds in your favor for success. And that makes it more likely you will take action, and continue to make decisions moving forward.

"Scratch the record" so that song will never play the same ever again. Like burning your ships.

Pour salt on your food.

Here's one way I've seen someone use the technique of burning your ships in everyday life. I have a friend who pours salt on her food once she has had enough to eat. Restaurants are famous for giving huge portions, so what she does after she has eaten enough is ruin the rest of it by pouring salt on it. Thus, she removes the temptation to eat more than she needs. This is just a simple way of illustrating how you can be intentional about what you really want.

Why decide?

Why should you decide? Why not just let things slide, and let others decide for me? Well, that is obviously one option. Just understand that by not making a proactive decision, you are making the decision not to decide. Decisions are a part of life and inevitable. You make them every day, whether you like it or not. Just like judging, we all do it, all the time, every day. For those of a more church-going background, the word "judging" has been thrown around and abused for decades, crippling men and women in making decisions.

Man looks at the outward appearance, but the Lord looks at the heart. In fact, one of the reasons Jesus was sent to Earth by God was to decide a matter and make a judgment.

"And Jesus said, "For judgment, I came into this world, so that those who do not see may see, and that those who see may become blind." John 9:39

Once you understand that decisions are inevitable, you begin to crystalize your thinking when you ask yourself why you allow others to decide for you.

One of my favorite movies is *Braveheart*, starring Mel Gibson who plays Scottish legend William Wallace. At the start of the movie, William is a young boy who just lost his father and brother in a battle against the English. Having no living family left in his village, his Uncle Argyle from another village arrives to pick up young William and take him back with him.

Immediately Uncle Argyle does two things. First, he is clear about his intentions. Second, he is clear about who is in charge. While eating a meal, he 'matter of factly' tells William, "We'll stay here tonight, and in the morning, you'll be coming back home with me."

To which young William replies, "I don't wanna go back with you."

Argyle flatly states, "You didn't want your father to die either, did ya? But it happened."

No debate, no raised voice, no coddling or apology. Just a clear, definite reply, conveying confidence, intention and power indicating in no uncertain terms "I am in charge here, got it?"

As the night goes on, William is fascinated by Uncle Argyle's massive sword. He's sad and angry that his father was killed, he is uncertain about the crazy uncle he just met, and he is confused about a lot of things. William feels like he needs to do something to avenge his father's and brother's death. That's why he is checking out his uncle's sword.

Argyle is aware of this and as William is touching the sword, Argyle gently pulls the sword away and taps young William on the forehead stating, "First learn to use this." Then he motions back to the sword and says, "Then I'll teach you to use this."

The message is clear, first learn to think and then learn to fight. You will need to do both in life. Think and fight.

> *"First learn how to think, then how to fight."*

https://youtu.be/8APUM-b4-ns

Here's another excellent historical example. Harriet Tubman was an American abolitionist and political activist. Born into slavery, Tubman escaped and subsequently made some 13 missions to rescue approximately 70 enslaved people, including family and friends, using the network of antislavery activists and safe houses known as the *Underground Railroad.*

She is quoted as saying, "I pray that I'll be strong enough to fight."

Pick your battles and pick the time to fight. You will need to do both throughout your life.

Principle #2: Choose What You Dwell On

Our mind is like a garden. If you see a beautiful garden that has been well maintained and full of flowers, fruits, and vegetables you can bet it didn't just happen that way. There is a gardener who took great care in developing that garden.

The gardener was careful to plant good seeds and then nurture them with fertilizer and water and plenty of sunshine. He kept out the bugs, the critters and picked the weeds at first sight, because he knows that weeds will choke out the good seeds.

He chose what to plant and what to kill off.

Our mind is like that. We choose what we allow to grow in our minds. We can't always choose what goes into our minds, but we can choose what we will let live. Be intentional about what you dwell on.

We all have had a number of experiences in our lives, some good some bad. You have likely experienced some tragedy and likely some great joy, too.

Depending on what you dwell on, you can change your mental state and future-outlook. If you choose to focus on the bad stuff, you will begin to think a certain way, looking for more bad stuff. Or you could choose the opposite and only think about the good. That, too, will affect your thinking and outlook. When you are feeling a little depressed and down about life, it is best to refocus on the good, the pure, the honorable, the lovely. You won't find it on the news or on social media. You have to go looking for it in good books, or my favorite, the *Bible*.

Windshield vs. Mirrors

Every car I have ever been in has a similar set up. There is a large front window and three small mirrors. The three small ones are the rearview mirror and the two side view mirrors. The window is massive compared to the size of the other three mirrors. The window is for looking at where you are going and the little mirrors are there for letting you know if something is coming up behind you or to see where you have been.

The size of these items is important to consider. The large window indicates that you should spend large amounts of time looking through the window, and where you are going. The small mirrors indicate that you should only glance at them. Yes, it is important to know where you came from, but it is much more important to know where you are going. If you dwell on the mirrors and don't pay attention to where you are going, you will crash.

Dwell on what you see out the big window, and only glance at the mirrors.

Focus Determines Direction

"The thoughts you keep in a loop determine the direction of your life." — Steven Furtick

We have a lot of thoughts every day. In fact, many experts believe we think somewhere between 60,000 and 80,000 thoughts per day. That averages out to 2,500 to 3,300 per hour. Remarkable, isn't it?
Thoughts are like seeds. Decide to nurture the ones you want, and decide to kill off or starve the ones you don't. Weeds or fruit? The choice is yours.

We have a guide to help us test our thoughts. Philippians 4:8 is a great test as to whether we should think about something:

> *"Finally, brethren, whatever is true, whatever is honorable, whatever is right, whatever is pure, whatever is lovely, whatever is of good repute, if there is any excellence and if anything worthy of praise, dwell on these things."* Philippians 4:8

The verse tells us to think about things that are true, noble, right, pure, lovely, admirable, excellent, and worthy of praise. Consider each word listed below:

Truth

Is it true? I will discuss the idea of truth in length later in the book, but for now, understand that there is truth and it can be known. I am not going to get into the metaphysical and obfuscate the obvious common sense understanding of what can be known. Things are true enough to make decisions, and the truth is known because it is self-evident. The truth is the way things actually are. It may not be politically correct to say this. In fact, it most certainly is not, politically correct.

Noble

Each and every one of us has a spark of the divine inside. We all have been given a touch of God. Our lives are on loan from God until He calls them back at some point. Because we are children of God, we're in the highest of ranks! Our thoughts should be royal and regal. Not in an arrogant way, but in not allowing ourselves to think in an unkind, timid, or repulsive manner. You are a child of the King and that makes you a prince or princess.
Think and act accordingly.

Right

You know the difference between right and wrong. So many people want to be right—to be the one who is never wrong. But too often we don't allow that desire for being right to permeate our thoughts. Thinking right thoughts means allowing accuracy and appropriateness to guide us. God created us with a knowledge of Him, but some men suppress that knowledge. You know right from wrong, so have the courage to follow it.

"His thoughts because that which is known about God is evident within them; for God made it evident to them." Romans 1:19

Pure

To be pure in heart and thought is not as difficult as it seems. It's simply choosing to think on ethical, good, upright, and honest things.

Lovely

This is a word that isn't used much, but it should be. To think lovely thoughts means to see the beautiful and stunning in life and allow our minds to think upon those things.

Admirable

To be admired is something most people want. But do we want admirable thoughts? Admirable thoughts are those that are credible and distinguished and allow us to live in such a way that is commendable.

Excellent

The best of the best is what excellent is. When our thoughts are excellent, they are superb, exceptional, and fabulous. Excellent thoughts lead us to live excellent lives.

Worthy of Praise

What thoughts are worthy of praise? Thoughts about God. His ways, His plans, and His creation, to name a few. It's safe to say that when our thoughts are on Him, that's a good thing.

We can test our thoughts every day. As we do this, eventually we won't have to test many of our thoughts because we will already know if they meet up to the standards

Intentional. Captured minds when marketing, be sure to capture your own thoughts. Which dog do you want to win the fight?

"Taking thoughts captive means controlling them instead of letting them control you." — Priscilla Shirer

My good friend Tony Rubleski has been teaching, coaching, and marketing for decades. He developed a phrase called "Captured Minds" for helping clients better develop marketing strategies for crystallizing thinking. He teaches business owners, speakers, and authors to capture more minds in this ever-increasing minefield of information overload. The best mind to capture, however, is your own!

I'm going to take a slight pause to discuss a big idea that some may find offensive. I want to apologize upfront, and if you don't like it, you don't have to read on, but I want to do a 20,000 foot view of the *Bible* and Christianity.

There is one book that has been printed more and more widely, and read more than any other in history, and that is the *Bible*. It is a history book, a song book, a poetry book, and it has been used for thousands of years.

Now, here is my point. Whether you believe that it is the Word of God or not doesn't matter. The point is that generations of people have looked at the *Bible* as the highest and most valuable document ever written down. The ideas, philosophies, and values for life have stood the test of time.

There have been countless people who have tried to discredit the *Bible*, and time and time again, through archaeology, and experience, the *Bible* stands tall as true.

Winston Churchill has a great quote about the truth. He says, "The truth is incontrovertible. Malice may attack it, ignorance may deride it, but in the end, there it is."

> *"The truth is incontrovertible. Malice may attack it, ignorance may deride it, but in the end, there it is." Winston Churchill*

I look at the *Bible* as the ultimate and highest form of literature. Nothing is higher than the Word of God. It stands supreme.

Likewise, Jesus Christ, is the ultimate man. He is also God. Thus, He gives us the only true guide on how to be human. The Son of God is the ultimate and highest being.

So, the best I can ever be, do or have is what Christ and the *Bible* have laid out as supreme. Those two - Jesus and the *Bible* - are consistent and clear standards to live by.

Here are some characteristics of God and the *Bible*:

True
All Powerful
All Knowing
Everywhere
Just
Loving

These are the highest standards to live by. I don't live up to them all the time, but they are there just the same and I know they are there. That is the standard. So, when I refer to the *Bible*, I am looking at the best, the straight line, the measuring stick for life. I will fall short, but that's part of life. I have to keep moving forward, keep making the best decisions that I can, and I can rest assured that "True North" is right there in front of me, guiding me. Knowing that True North is there, and not measuring up to it is different than denying that True North even exists.

It's like a compass. I can study the compass. I can focus and dwell on the compass to guide my ship. I will get off course sometimes. Because of the compass, I know when I am off course, and I can correct my actions by making adjustments. That is far different than denying the compass even exists, or has any value at all. Without a determined commitment to the compass, the truth, you will be destined to hug the shore. But, to the person who knows and trusts in the compass, he can sail all over the world.

That is how I view the *Bible* and Jesus Christ. They are the compass, the True North, my guiding principles for life. I have looked, tested and experienced other writing, but only the *Bible* stands the test of time. So I use the *Bible* as the highest standard, my compass. Then I use my logic and reason applied to experience and evidence to wisely make decisions. This process has served me well. I truly believe it is the only way to make wise decisions.

To use this method, I have to have some idea of what the *Bible* actually says. So I spend a little bit of time every day reading it for myself.

Principle #3: Capture Your Mind

First, be intentional about what you nurture, and what you allow into your mind. Take each thought, capture it, and see how it lines up with the *Bible*. Is it true, just, diligent, honorable, etc.?

"We are destroying speculations and every lofty thing raised up against the knowledge of God, and we are *taking every thought captive* to the obedience of Christ." 2 Corinthians 10:5

Second, be wise. There are evil people in the world, and there are also stupid or naive people in the world. The evil ones will try and trip you up on purpose. They may deceive you, or maybe not. But they want to harm you for whatever reason. Then there are the naive. They may mean good for you, but their advice is faulty and off base, leading to pain. Your job is to test everything and judge right from wrong. Use the *Bible* as the standard; not the tradition of men, not philosophy, and not simple principles of the world.

"See to it that no one takes you captive through philosophy and empty deception, according to the tradition of men, according to the elementary principles of the world, rather than according to Christ." Colossians 2:8

Chapter Four

Why Is It Sometimes So Hard to Decide?

If you have 20 decisions to make, each with only two outcomes, you have over 1 million total possible outcomes. That can be overwhelming to think about. Add to it that we make over 5,000 decisions each day, and you can see why decision making can be intimidating.

Define the Word

Remember, decide means to "cut away." It literally means to eliminate options. Eliminating options is both risky and freeing, because once you make that decision your thinking becomes clearer. You now have fewer options to choose from.

Decide to Eliminate Options

Once you decide to do something, the battle is half won. Decide how healthy you want to be. Decide what kind of relationships you want. Decide to become the kind of man or woman you want to be.

Once you decide, you eliminate the other decisions and simplify your life. Without a clear, definiteness of purpose, anything is available. This actually means nothing is available, because you haven't decided what you want.

So, start with some big hairy audacious decisions, like your health. Decide how healthy you want to be mentally, spiritually and physically, and then decide how to make it happen. You will inevitably adjust your course after you begin making decisions, and that's okay. In fact, that's how it should be.

Accept the Risks

It is known that people have trouble making decisions when they are depressed. In fact, chronic indecisiveness is so common that it is considered diagnostically important and is mentioned in the latest version of the Diagnostic and Statistical Manual of Mental Disorders (DSM-5) – the book in which mental illnesses, like depression, are defined. People with depression both avoid decision-making and tend to be slower when making decisions.

Gain perspective by being curious and pay attention and test everything except sex. That area is one where personal experience is best to hold sacred due to the effects it has on your mind, body, and yes, your spirit.

Keep it in perspective. I hate to burst your bubble, but the reality, nobody really cares as much as you do. So, don't let the opinions of others affect your indecision.

Turn it into an adventure. Intentionally get lost and try to find your way home. Intentionally put yourself in a position where you know nothing at all and try to figure it out. These little "tests" of your ability will do two things, it will give you some newfound confidence about your abilities, and will also help you realize, through experience, that it wasn't really all that bad.

Tim Ferriss, the bestselling author and entrepreneur,

recommends trying what he calls "Comfort Zone Challenges" for a number of different reasons. They can help you build confidence and also convince you that what might seem impossible at first is actually fully achievable.

Okay, so you're not going to lay down in a Starbucks, fair enough. You can do other "outside of your comfort zone" things to start building confidence and overcoming indecision. There is really no better way to fully realize "it's not that important" by trying it, when it really is "not that important." For example, here are a few things you can try today:

Interacting with Strangers-The four guys in *Yes Theory* make a living out of their uncomfortable interactions with strangers (check out their popular YouTube channel).

Try Something New-Try something that goes against your own perception of yourself. If you can't cook take a cooking class. Unathletic? Hire a trainer. I was told for years that I couldn't write. I still don't think I'm that good and yet, I do it anyway. As Jordan Peterson says, "You have to be willing to be a fool before you can be a hero." Nobody starts as an expert, so try something new and get started today!

Be Han Solo and Go It Alone-Have you ever gone to the movies or restaurant alone? What about a vacation? I know, the thought of doing those things may scare you out of your mind, worrying about what people are saying about you, etc. But, that is exactly the point. Do it anyway, as an experiment, and see what happens. Be confident, be bold, hold your head high, and go for it!

It's all about taking something that makes you nervous, flipping it around and drawing newfound confidence from it in a safe yet seemingly dangerous way. It's not dangerous, it just feels like it is. Then, once you do a few of those things and realize it wasn't all that bad (or maybe it was and you still did it anyway) you have just added a little bit to your "confidence reservoir" so you will be better equipped to handle other things. You have the experience of overcoming a small amount of adversity and you can draw from that and use it for future adverse circumstances.

So, take a safe, scary and silly risk today, and let the decision-making begin!

We do not fail for lack of information, we fail for a lack of judgment, and discernment.

And remember, there is a lot of information, and there are many conflicting viewpoints. We are in an Information Age. Information is all around us and available at an ever-increasing rate. We do not fail for lack of information, we fail for a lack of judgment, and discernment. Why? Because we fail to teach how to discern right from wrong and good and evil. Truth is the way things are. Logic and reason applied to evidence.

False hope is the idea or belief in an outcome that has no chance of happening. False hope is a result of faulty belief. Faulty beliefs are based on wishes, they are not based in reality or fact. To make good decisions you have to commit your mind to the truth. Wishing something to be a certain way and ignoring the facts do not lead to sound decision making.

Why do society and the church teach people not to judge? Do they really mean never make a decision, or never make a choice? Really, when you think about it, it means don't think, or more specifically, don't think for yourself. Check your logic, reason, and discernment at the door, and we'll tell you what to think and what to believe.

When you have non-thinking, compliant followers they are much easier to control. They don't take much initiative and might not be all that creative, but they are more manageable. Don't be that person! Think, decide, and act.

Chapter Five

Know The Recipe for Dumb Decision-Making (So You Can Avoid It)

Ingredient #1: Make emotionally-based decisions. Wise decisions are made with your brain, not emotions or feelings. It's called critical thought and it requires, truth, logic, and reason based on the way things actually are.

But, using your head to lead doesn't mean you don't care. It means you are making a better decision based on the available information.

When my youngest daughter Natalie wanted to leave the house on a Sunday, the rule was, no leaving the house until your room was clean. Well, she didn't have any plans, so, why clean the room?

You can guess what happened. Her friend called to say they were going to the movies and a cute boy she was interested in was going to be there too!

Natalie bounded from her room and excitedly exclaimed, "Dad, were going to the movies and guess who's going to be there!?"

"I'm sorry sweetie, you're not going anywhere until your

room is clean."

Tears welling up inside, Natalie whimpered, "But Dad! You don't understand!"

Tears streaming down her face.

I coolly replied, "Natalie, you're the youngest of four children. Tears stopped working on me years ago. Clean your frickin' room."

Sniffing, she replied, "Okay, Dad."

You might be thinking that's a little tough. After all, it's just a room and it's just a movie, what's the big deal? Just let her go. And you'd be wrong.

Children need discipline, rules and order and that comes from me, Dad. She needs to know that emotionalism and tears don't make the decisions, I do.

It's similar to when someone you love says, "If you loved me you would x, y, or z."
That's not love; that's extortion.

Emotions are like the motor on a boat. The emotions give you energy and motivation but it's the rudder, your brain, the critical thinking utilizing data, logic, reason and truth that guide your actions. Without the rudder, the boat will just spin around in the middle of the lake, but once the rudder is engaged, you can guide that boat to

When making a decision that feels a little too emotional, pretend you are making the decision for someone else.

wherever you want to go.

When making a decision that feels a little too emotional, pretend you are making the decision for someone else. One of the best ways to put your emotions in the right place is to imagine you are making the decision for your child.

Ask, "what would you tell your son or daughter to do?"

Ingredient #2: Allow yourself to be deceived. The classic story of deception is when the serpent intentionally deceived Eve with the fruit of the knowledge of good and evil. The serpent was crafty and told her of all the great things that would happen if she took the fruit and ate. She thought it was the wise thing to do. She was trying to help her family by doing the right thing. She saw that it looked good, so she took it and ate the fruit.

Then, she gave it to her husband Adam. She wasn't trying to deceive him. She thought it was a good thing to do. Adam knew it was wrong, but he did it anyway.

This story illustrates that women are more likely than men to be deceived, but men are more capable of evil.

The serpent had an evil motive, Eve had a good motive.

<u>Motives</u>

"All the ways of a man are clean in his own sight, But the LORD weighs the motives."

Motives are tricky things. Where do they come from? They come from desire, which is a result of what we see. I believe, at the bedrock of every desire is a positive God-ordained longing. The problem lies with how we try to fulfill that desire.

For example, take money. Wanting money, using money, and having money are fine. Money represents security, power, position, etc. You get the idea. Security, position, and power are all good desires, and deciding to utilize them is fine.

Money on its own is amoral. It isn't good or bad. It is neutral. It is the character and motive of the man that determines whether money will be used for good or evil. It is kind of like a brick. The brick can be used to build a hospital, or you can throw the brick through a window. Same brick, two different outcomes.

Check your motives, because they can be tricky things. Never underestimate the power we have to delude ourselves. Especially in a free country like the USA, everything is available today. But be sure to count the costs!

Ingredient #3: Fail to decide. "When I try to take responsibility, I hit one rejection after another. It is easier to just let things slide."

Can you relate to this sentiment? I can. I remember when I first graduated from college and had my first job. I would start to save a little bit of money and then, Wham! Car trouble, or an emergency would pop up, something always seemed to happen once I started making some headway. It felt like that "Whack-A-Mole" game where the moles keep popping up, and I have to keep hitting them down.

Then it dawned on me. When I took responsibility, I was swimming against the stream, and I wasn't used to it. But once you start swimming, you will get stronger. Keep going. Don't wish it were easier, wish you were better.

Whack the mole! They will keep coming and the bigger and better you get, the bigger the moles will become. Just keep on whacking those moles!

Psychologist Carl Jung said, "Man needs difficulties; they are necessary for health."

"The greatest and most important problems of life are all in a certain sense insoluble. They must be so because they express the necessary polarity inherent in every self-regulating system. They can never be solved, but only outgrown."

Read that again. Problems must be outgrown. Therefore, you must grow. In other words, don't wish there were no more problems - wish you were better.

The other option is to just go with the flow like a dead fish.

That's why we live in America, the freedom and liberty to make a decision, and choose our own path. We are the only country ever founded on the basis that freedom comes from God. We are also the only nation separating the church and the state. That's one thing that makes AMERICA unique and great. The value of the individual is infinitely greater than the worth of the state.

Anxiety comes upon us when we can't decide where to go, who to see, or what to do we put ourselves in a state of anxiety. Too many options to choose from so we don't decide, and we are left feeling anxious. Or which way things are about to go.

It is only when you come to the realization that it really doesn't matter, that you begin to understand the superficiality of it all. You see, it doesn't really matter in the long term what you choose, because there is no negative without the positive, and no positive without the negative.

Ingredient #4: Don't Hold Yourself Accountable. Do not hold yourself accountable or even check the results. Maybe you can let things slide for one day, one week but a year? No, that's too long. The fourth major ingredient for dumb decision making is a lack of accountability. It's what I call the "Let it Slide" attitude.

I see this attitude, dare I say arrogance?, in the current "OK, Boomer" reply when an older person offers some type of advice or feedback. When I was growing up, there was a popular movie called *Logan's Run*. It is a cult classic with the primary message that anyone over 30-years old wasn't just not to be listened to, there were to be exterminated and killed in a public celebration called "carrousel." Don't trust anyone over 30 was a popular mantra.

The problem is that by eliminating the input from people over 30, you are severely limiting your availability to healthy and wise input. This is a common short coming of the younger generation and I was no different at that age. Teenagers and 20-somethings tend to think that the old folks are out of touch and don't have a clue about what life is really like, when in actuality, the old folks have been around the block and are honestly trying to help the young so they don't make the same dumb mistakes they did.

Look at it this way. If you are 26 years old, how would you respond to a 13-year-old instructing you on the ways of the world? How do you think a 52-year-old would reply to you as a 26-year-old? Are you smarter than you were 4 years ago? 10 years ago?

It is true that the "boomers" may be stuck in their ways and maybe rigid in their thinking, but it is a result of experience and what works and what is important in life. It's good to test and challenge traditions and norms, but before utterly destroying a tradition, you better have something better to replace it with. Don't destroy a tradition just because you don't like it, and fail to replace it with a better one. The traditions are there for a reason, they work.

Go ahead and make decisions, test and challenge, but check the results right away. Now clearly, you're not going to plant a seed in the spring and on May 1st quit your garden if there is nothing to eat. It takes some time for a vegetable garden to grow. But you can check the progress, and make adjustments, if needed. Is it getting enough light, are the bugs attacking the garden, too much water, not enough? You make mid-course corrections.

But, when someone says they will do something by a specific time and it doesn't get done, you should start taking notice and start a contingency plan. Don't hesitate either. As Brian Tracy says in his book "Eat That Frog." If you have to eat a frog, get it over with and just do it!

Hesitation leads to more pain. Take intentional action. Letting things slide will not make it better, only worse. Stay accountable. Some of you are good at holding yourself accountable, others, not so much. As Plato and Socrates taught, "know yourself." Knowing yourself is a key ingredient to successful decision making. Know your shortcomings, your strengths, and weaknesses, and be open to feedback. Even a scumbag that doesn't have your best interest at heart can have valuable insight to your character and how he sees the world you live in. Listen, accept it, and judge the value and merits of the insight he offers, then take the good and leave the bad.

I once knew a man who was hyper critical. A very wise man indeed, but his criticisms could be biting at times. He was one of the early leaders of the Toyota, just-in-time, one-piece-flow inventory management philosophy, and taught college course across the country long before the automotive industry did.

Now, as for you non-business, and non-manufacturing people, basically, what he did was show businesses how to generate higher cash flow and profits, by simply changing how they manufactured their products. It resulted in massive cash flow improvement, and financial viability for companies. It was truly cutting-edge thinking.

Well, I knew the value of his insight. He wasn't perfect, none of us are, but he was wise. And I believe he had my best interest at heart. However, he was hyper critical. I think that came from his way of thinking and processing things. I'm not sure where it came from, but it didn't really matter where it came from, it was just there.

By the way, as a side note. You don't have to know why things are the way they are. You just have to know that they are that way. Don't ask "why is he a jackass?" Just know that he is, and act accordingly. It is better to ask "who" rather than "why?" You don't have to know how a tree produces fruit, juts pick the fruit and enjoy the apple. It's a helpful shortcut.

Anyway, this guy was a very critical man. Loving, kind, wise, but critical nonetheless. Well, I remember one summer day at our cottage where he was ripping into me about something. It went on for a while. I listened, I asked clarifying questions and not once did I tell him to "F-off" or "get lost." I just listened and learned. I learned his insight, I learned his perception of me, and I learned how he thought.

It was very helpful. After his tirade ended, his wife came into the kitchen and asked why I put up with that kind of abuse.

I told her that I think he is wise, I think he loves me, and I think he has my best interest at heart. If I tell him to shut up or stop, then I will also stop the flow of unfiltered feedback that I see as invaluable. Once that stops, I lose valuable information to help me get better.

She incredulously said, "I would never do that or put up with that."

Well, that tells me more about her than about me.

Strong, confident, humble, and wise people want feedback. They want insight and perspectives that are different from their own beliefs. That is what humility is. Knowing that other people's insights and opinions and perspectives have value. Humble people listen and learn. Arrogant people don't. After all, why should they? They know it all anyway.

That is another reason why we pray. Praying confirms our humility. Praying is the tangible evidence that we admit we are not in control and that we don't know it all. We admit that there is a higher power, a Being larger and more knowing than we are. Prayer admits our own shortcomings and is an attempt to align with Something bigger than ourselves. Prayer epitomizes and personifies humility.

Getting harsh feedback can be tough to hear. It's hard. But, most things of value are hard and tough. Saving $1 million is hard, marriage is hard, raising children, starting a business, paying off debt are all hard to do. But they are valuable, and they are worth it. Don't be afraid of the hard things, they make you grow.

But only the secure can be humble. That is why it is important to build a reservoir of strength and confidence on a regular basis, so you cannot simply withstand the difficulty, but thrive in it. Start your day with the good, the pure, the positive and nurture those attitudes and beliefs daily. Cultivate friendships with good men and women who will speak truth and kindness and offer a safe haven where you both can build each other up and stay accountable. Mental health is a key place to start!

Our own personal physical health is also good place to hold ourselves accountable too. We might be able to get away with a few extra pounds for a few extra years. But you get over 20 pounds and you had better start to take some action. Don't fool yourself into thinking you can get away with it because you cannot fool your body. Yeah, you might be able to fool me and your friends or coworkers, but your body is keeping score and keeping track.

Ingredient #5: Pride: "I Know Better." With regard to accountability, men have a particular blind spot. We don't like asking for directions, and we don't like to be told what to do. We think we know better, and when we make a decision we tend to let them go longer than need be believing that if we just put in a few more dollars or a little more time, etc., it will all work out.

You can't rescue a bad decision. You will need to change course or cut bait and chalk it up as a "learning experience." Early detection and early correction are the mantra. Hold yourself and others accountable by checking the results against the plan and then make the necessary adjustments right away.

One of my earlier business ventures, in my arrogance, I believed that I could overcome any adversity. Right from the start sales were not even close to projections. But I was assured that they would come. So, I invested more money. Sales picked up, slightly, and again I was assured that they will come, so I invested more money. Ten years roll by and I'm running out of money to keep investing, and then make one last major investment to make it work, that's when the banking crisis of 2008/2009 hit, and the economy just came to a halt.

Now, not only did I use all of my liquid cash, but I also had $500,000 in debt. The bottom line-bankruptcy! Not a pleasant experience at all.

Fast forward to a country club investment I got involved in five years later. The plan was $100,000 investment that would return 5x the amount in three years once the club was turned around.

But it did not start well, and when numbers weren't what they were supposed to be, so I got personally involved to oversee the operation. Eighteen months into the project, with many broken promises and lackluster results, I pulled the plug. Yes, I lost my investment. But I didn't lose more than that.

About a year after that experience, I told one of my Uber passengers that story. They were executives from the Dallas area. They told me that they were actually thinking about starting a consulting firm to talk men out of buying country clubs because the average loss is $400,000! Yes, I lost money, but not nearly that much!

The bottom line is to check the results early and often and take appropriate action immediately.

Chapter Six

The Relationship Between Decision-Making, Control, and Anxiety

We can work to make good decisions. We can't avoid all bad decisions. I certainly haven't. Good or bad, however, the simple act of making decisions will simplify your life and start to eliminate anxiety. The best we can do is to decide and then make mid-course corrections.

It's time to get comfortable with deciding. Start by taking a different way home. Try and figure it out by getting lost. Get creative and see what you can do to figure it out.

Choose what to dwell on.

Summarizing Philippians 4:6-10, it reminds us that Whatever is true, honorable etc., dwell on these, and the God of peace will be with you.

When we fill our thoughts with the right things, the wrong ones must struggle to get in!

Fill up on junk food or fruits and veggies? Feed my dog brussel sprouts?

In the same vein, you might know Paul's exhortation in Colossians 3:2 NIV: "Set your mind on things above, not on earthly things." In setting our minds on "things above" we will have less thoughts that need testing and being taken captive.

Be intentional about who you are around, and what you put into your mind. You are the average of the 5 people you spend the most time with. Ask yourself: "Is that ok?" Is that taking you closer to, or farther from your goal?

Cut things out that do not help.

"Therefore, since we have so great a cloud of witnesses surrounding us, let us also lay aside every encumbrance, and the sin, which so easily entangles us, and let us run with endurance, the race that is set before us." Hebrews 12:1

If you choose to dwell on those things that do not help, then you have chosen to not have the peace that comes from God. The decision is yours.

So how can you discern between those things that help and those that do not? Consider the following...

Desire or Greed?

Desire for things, for the most part, is good. Greed, on the other hand, is not. There is an invisible line that separates the two. I'm not sure where you cross it, but it is there.

Maybe desires turn into greed when you sacrifice things like your family or friendships in the pursuit of something. That is why goal setting, although good for getting out of a chaotic mess, must be tempered. Goals can become a drug and filter out everything else in your life. Which can be a good thing, but be aware of how they are affecting you, and your relationships.

Naive or Toxic?

"It doesn't really matter; it's out of my control anyway. What's the point?"

Well, you do have 100% control, and not to think so is naive. Not thinking so also results in an unrealistic and fatalistic view of your life that often leads to depression.

Born in 1842, American Psychologist William James, known as the "Father of Modern Psychology," was part of a prominent family. He was well-educated and had successful siblings, but as a young adult, William was suicidal for months on end. This was the result of believing that his life was futile and that he had no control over what his life would be. His religious upbringing taught him that God was in control and that we were basically destined to the "fate" that God had for us.

This idea so captured James' mind that he actually had a gun and was sitting on the waterfront where he contemplated ending it all.

But he had an idea. Before he would end it all, he would try and experiment with his life. After all, if it didn't matter anyway, why not try something new? He set out on a mindset of 100% absolute control over his life. He would believe that he was the master of his fate and that he alone controlled his life.

He became a professor at Harvard, he got married, and eventually became known as the Father of Psychology, dying at age 68, 40 years later, of heart disease.

In the book *Power of Habit,* author Charles Duhigg

concludes:

"Once we choose *(DECIDE)* who we want to be, people grow to the way in which they have been exercised . . . If you believe you can change, if you make it a habit, the change becomes real. This is the real power of habit. The insight that your habits are what you choose them to be. Once that choice occurs, and becomes automatic, habitual, it's not only real, it starts to seem inevitable."

"And once you understand that habits can change, you have the *freedom* and the *responsibility* to remake them. Once you understand that habits can be rebuilt, the power of habit becomes easier to grasp, and the only option left is to get to work."

"Habits are the compound interest of self-improvement." James Clear author of Atomic Habits

Likewise, bad habits are the compound interest of self-destruction.

You have absolute control. The psychiatrist William James was suicidal. But, as his one last experiment before he killed himself, he DECIDED to live as if he had total control.

"Once you understand that habits can change, you have the freedom and the responsibility to remake them . . . Once you understand that habits can be rebuilt, the power of habit becomes easier to grasp and the only option left is to get to work." William James

Extreme ownership. Own it. Don't blame. Because you are owned by whoever or whatever you blame. Don't let anyone or anything own you.

"But Robert, it's not my fault!"

Maybe that's true, however, be very careful with that mindset. Even if it is true that someone intentionally screwed you over and took advantage of you, own it anyway. There is always something you could have done to protect yourself or prevent it from happening.

Even if it is true that someone intentionally screwed you over and took advantage of you, own it anyway.

The problem with NOT owning the situation is that you are no longer in control. And that puts someone else in charge. In other words, they own you and your life. YOU take control. YOU own it ALL. That way, you are the author of your fate.

Now, I know that there are things in life that you can't control, like 9/11 planes flying into the World Trade Towers, tornadoes, and earthquakes. But you have much more control than you think you have. Whatever you can control, take charge, and take care of it. You have both the freedom and responsibility to remake your life.

But the question still remains, the freedom and responsibility to remake them into *WHAT?* Without a meaning or definite purpose, it really doesn't matter, does it? But it is really that simple. Or as Andy Dufresne stated in *The Shawshank Redemption*, "It really comes down to this, get busy living or get busy dying."

Don't kill yourself, but live like you were dying. Because you are.

In Dr. David DeWitt's book *The Mature Man*, he states, "in order for a boy to become a man, he must turn his chaos into order. A child thinks and acts like a child." He reasons, "Why clean my room if it's going to get messy again anyway? What's the point? Well, the point is to become a man and men take responsibility and turn chaos into order. Making your bed and cleaning your room is a simple task that can be made into a habit that takes no thought at all once the habit is established."

You get to choose your habits, and then your habits choose who you will become. So, be intentional about what habits rule your life. You do have the power to change them if you desire, and if you decide to.

Chapter Seven

The Recipe For Wise Decision-Making (So You Can Be the Author of Your Life)

Ingredient #1: Choose What to Decide. It is true that you have 100% control over your life, yes, you do. But it is also true that fate, or chance, or consequences also have 100% over your life. Wait, what? How can those both be true? Well, they are. How can a circle also be a triangle? Well, they can't, unless of course it is a cone, then it makes perfect sense, depending on your perspective.

The academic word for this apparent dichotomy is an antinomy. It means two opposing ideas that coincide together.

CK Chesterton had a great way of describing his Christian faith. **"A glad and angry faith."** That's what he called it. Huh, "glad" and "angry?" Those two words don't seem to fit, but they do.

The beaver in *The Lion, the Witch, and the Wardrobe* said this about God:

"Safe?! Who ever said anything about 'safe? He isn't safe, but He's good."

Huh? How could someone who is good not be safe? For some reason my dentist comes to mind. Dr. Brennan is the best dentist in Grand Rapids. I've told him many times how much I hate him, and that's exactly why I come every six months so he can check my teeth. I want him to catch whatever he is going to catch early!

But, when he pulls out his needle and follows it right behind with a drill, he has perverse grin when he says, "RJ, this is going to hurt."

No candy coating, no negotiation. It is going to hurt. Is that safe? I don't think so! But it is good. It is right and it is the wise thing to do.

I need to work and take responsibility for every part that I can control like it is entirely up to me. Then I need to pray fervently like it is entirely up to God. But it is good to take stock into what you can and cannot control. Know yourself, and take stock of your life.

Here are some examples of what you can and cannot control.

You can't choose the country in which you were born.
You can't choose who your parents are.
You can't choose your family.
You can't choose the past.

You can decide on your attitude.
You can decide your direction.
You can decide who you love.

Ingredient #2: Be a Velvet-Covered Brick. A great metaphor to kind in mind is a velvet-covered brick. They seem like polar opposites that could never be joined together, but they need to be. Be easy to talk with and get along with (that's the velvet) but be firm in principles, make the tough decisions and stick with them (that's the brick).

> *Be easy to talk with and get along with (that's the velvet) but be firm in principles, make the tough decisions and stick with them (that's the brick).*

Another apparent dichotomy is faith and wisdom.

Faith and wisdom are connected. Well, at least they should be, if they are not, it's not faith, it's a wish, a superstition, a dream or a whim. Likely it's simply a distraction keeping you from what you ought to be doing.

The difference between faith and superstition is that the first uses reason to go as far as it can, and then makes the jump; the second shuns reason entirely — which is why superstition is not the ally, but the enemy, of true religion.
Sidney J Harris

Faith is not "blind faith" or "wishful thinking." Faith applies logic and reason to the evidence available. For example, I have faith that the airplane will get me from Grand Rapids to Houston to see my son. I can't guarantee that I will get there until I get there. But my logic and reason weigh the evidence, the safety records, the schedules, and determining that it is a wise thing to do. Yes, we could crash, or the plane could get diverted and we end up in Austin instead. But that is an example of good faith or wisdom.

Supreme Court Justice Clarence Thomas was recently quoted at Hillsdale College saying, "Faith and Wisdom are mutually reinforcing."

I think this idea has been lost on a generation (or more) of people. There is this faulty idea about faith that it is not based on wisdom, evidence or reason and logic. Faith is just faith, it's just something you believe to be true void of any evidence or logic or reason. That is the farthest thing from the truth. That kind of "faith" is just stupid. Yet, we teach it at a young age to children.

Ho, Ho, Ho! Every Christmas, parents teach their children to be good because Santa Claus is coming to town. We teach children to believe in Santa Claus. We teach them to believe in nonsense. Now, that may seem like just good clean fun and part of the Christmas season experience. But, do you still believe in Santa Claus? Why not?

Because he isn't real. It's make-believe. No sane, rational, wise or mentally sound person believes in Santa Claus. Yet, this is how we have defined the word "faith" or "belief."

If your faith and beliefs are not grounded in evidence, testimony, logic, reason and critical thinking, then it's just stupid. It's time to wake up and smell the pop tarts.

Ingredient #3: Decide to Decide. You may be asking yourself, what you should decide? The first thing to keep in mind is what you have the ability to decide and what you don't. You can't choose who your parents are, where you were born, the era in which you were born or your gender. But you do have unlimited decisions to make that are all at your discretion.

Yes, the list of options is infinite and one decision, although will eliminate some choices, it will also open up others to you.

Ingredient #4: Consistently be Humble, Hungry and Smart. You probably can't beat Jeff Bezos, LeBron James or Post Malone in their areas of expertise. What about someone local that you know and admire? Pick an area you enjoy or interests you and start there. Pop Warner, 10-year-old football player's don't compete against Tom Brady, and LeBron James isn't ever going to be a professional jockey racing horses at Keenland, KY.

Decide to . . .
Be humble
Be meek
Be truthful
Be diligent
Be strong
Be wise
Be a good steward
Be a fighter and a peacemaker.
Be optimistic

Attitude

"Any fact facing us, however difficult, even seemingly hopeless, is not so important as our attitude toward that fact," Norman Vincent Peale

Attempt

Decide to try. Remember Jesus' parable of talents. He was ok with the results of the men who tried but, he was ticked off at the guy who didn't even try. Y'all have talents. Some have more than you and some have less. To whom each is given from each will be required. Five does five more, two does two. Application: do something with your talents that will add value. AND don't miss the "why!" Why do it? Self-interest.

Debt

The *Bible* teaches that the borrower is a slave to the lender. Do you want to be a slave? Me neither, so stay out of debt. If you're in debt, get out, like a gazelle being chased by a lion, get out fast!

By the way, some of the best material for personal finance can be found at Dave Ramsey. He has free tools to help with budgeting, investing, getting out of debt, and becoming wealthy. Google him and watch his free YouTube videos for your own personal finance development. He is the best.

Ingredient #5: Choose Who or What You Will Serve. We all see the world through a grid or a prism of values. We have an idea of what is valuable and what is not. These values determine goals or targets to shoot for, and we prioritize them based on how we perceive them to align with what we value.

For example, if I see popularity and respect as important, and I enjoy golf. I may choose to spend lots of time perfecting my golf game and becoming a scratch golfer. I will have lots of requests for playing on golf teams due to my booming drives off the tee, and soft hands that darn near make putt on every green. I will earn the respect of the country club golfers, and gain popularity by being asked to play regularly with others.

But golf is a fickle and demanding sport, especially if you want to be a scratch golfer. By setting that goal, I eliminate the ability to spend lost time with my children, my business and others. And that may be OK. Just know that your values determine your goals.

In the *Bible*, Joshua is talking with his fellow countryman and says the same thing. Choose today whom you will serve. If it is disagreeable for you to serve the God of the *Bible*, decide what is important and stop monkeying around with nonsense.

Choose for yourself whom you will serve and then do it.

"If it is disagreeable in your sight to serve the LORD, choose for yourselves today whom you will serve: whether the gods which your fathers served which were beyond the River, or the gods of the Amorites in whose land you are living; but as for me and my house, we will serve the LORD." Joshua 24:15

My priorities were the *Bible*, wife, children, friends, work, etc. in that order. Now that my wife divorced me, that list no longer includes her (lol).

I knew my marriage was really over when after I had jumped through a thousand different hoops for her, and it still wasn't enough. I finally asked, "What is it you want from me? I can't seem to win with you."

Her reply, "I want you to get on your knees and beg me to stay."

It reminded me of the movie *300* when Leonidas was asked to bow down and worship the bad king. Leonidas said, you see that is a difficult thing for us Spartans. We don't do that. We made our decision long ago in fact to never do that. We have chosen who we will serve, and it is not you. So, when my wife asked me to get on my knees and beg her to stay, well, that was a problem because my decision had been made long before I even met her.

I am not a perfect man, far from it, but I will not bow-down to another human being, ever. I have chosen to serve the Lord of the *Bible* and Him only. He takes first place, then my wife, then my children, then work, etc.

So, when she said that, I knew it was over. She was never my wife. Her god was security, control, power, and domination, and she saw money as the vehicle to get her that.

I had made my commitment long ago. My priorities were straight and true. The Compass was sound. I'm not always perfect with the Compass, but I know where it is and where it was pointing. And it doesn't point to worshipping people.

William Wallace was asked in prison to renounce his beliefs, and he chose instead to die for them. What are you willing to die for? What sacrifice are you willing to make?

Find those things, choose them, and get busy living.

If you don't have any beliefs worth dying for, what then? All we have to give is our attention, or where we focus our efforts. No fool is he, who gives something he can never keep, to gain something he can never lose. Trading your time for low-level things is depressing. Pursuing pleasures at the expense of real value isn't much better.

Stand for something or you will fall for anything. One of my favorite movie clips is from Scent of a Woman, with Christopher O'Donnell and Al Pacino.

Nothing worse than an amputated spirit. There is no prosthetic for that.

Watch this from *Scent of a Woman:*

https://youtu.be/Xq8CtJSQFL4

And this: *Lands, titles, men, power . . . nothing.*
https://youtu.be/QGsggAK118w

Get enough information then pull the trigger and test it. Then refine your aim and pull the trigger again. Keep trying and keep on keeping on.

He came to bring true light and life to men.

My case for the *Bible*: The Apostle Paul challenges us at the beginning of Romans 12 to "not conform to the pattern of this world but be transformed by the renewing of our minds." The Greek word for the word renewing is *ananeosi,* and it literally means renovation.

When a house is old, outdated or a mess you put it through a renovation to revive it and renew. Your mind is similar and needs constant updates. Your mind is more powerful than an iPhone or super-computer, and just like your smart phone needs continual software updates, so does your mind. The software version of you in 3rd grade will not support you effectively when your 33, 43, or 53. You need to be updating your "software" with true, honorable, and good things.

That doesn't mean you skip the bad, awful and tragic things, but it seems that the good, the pure, and honorable things tend to get drowned out by the ugly. The old saying in the news is "if it bleeds it leads" so, the things that shout from the rooftops are typically the bad. The things that go "viral" online typically are not the things that will help you achieve massive amounts of success in life.

Every automobile I have driven in has a rearview mirror and two side mirrors so I can see what is coming up behind me and to a lesser extent, to see where I have been. The windshield, in contrast is huge compared to the tiny mirrors. There is wisdom in that.

When you drive, you tend to go where you are looking. Kind of like goals. You set a goal and your mind will start working toward achieving it. Now, the windshield is big, expansive, and in front of you. The mirrors, on the other hand are small, narrow and looking behind you. What's the point? Well, the point is that if you spend too much time looking at things behind you that have already happened, and ignore what is going on in front of you, and where you are going, you will crash, and you will not achieve your destination.

If you never look behind you, then you may miss out on some learning and even get caught off guard by someone coming up behind you, like a competitor in business. You want to pay attention to both what's in front of you, and what is behind you. BUT you want to spend a LOT more time looking ahead of you than looking behind you. Glance at what is behind you, and gaze on what is in front of you. 80/20 rule perhaps is good to keep in mind. Spend 80% looking ahead, goals and where you are going, and then no more than 20% in review, pondering and remembering.

Be intentional and decide what to focus on, for that will eventually determine what you get.

Chapter Eight

Choose Your Health

Health is more than your body fat percentage or even how you feel physically. It's physical, yes, and it's mental, emotional, and spiritual. So you have choices to make in each of these areas. How healthy physically do you want to be? How mentally well? How wise? It's also relational.

Here's how I do it. I ask myself the following questions. Then I assert my will over my emotions and over that which I can control in my circumstances. Next I make a choice that I believe moves me toward my goal, and finally I act according to my choices so that I achieve my goals.

How Healthy Do You Want To Be?

How healthy do you want to be? Decide. Do you want to be able to wake up every day with a spring in your step or foggy and hungover? Are you sick and tired of being sick and tired? Create little habits to eliminate other decisions. Set your workout clothes out the night before. Commit to a buddy that you will join him at the gym. Make a bet with Runbet.com and wager an amount of money to "force" your commitment.

Decide what you want, and then commit to it by setting up ways to make it easier to commit than not too.

That is one reason why trainers and coaches are so important.

You will get results just by making a decision, and starting a health program, but you will get much better results when you hire and use a personal trainer or coach. The same is true for business coaching or personal coaching. Sure, you can look up YouTube videos and learn how to fix your car, or do your taxes, or maybe even defend yourself in a court of law. But the use of a professional not only gives you access to their expertise, it also gives you accountability, to actually get done what you what to get done.

You don't have to use a trainer or a coach forever. Set a 90-day plan, or a one-year plan to have them help you set goals, make decisions and help you learn. Then you can choose to continue to use them or not. Take a break and see how it goes, check your results and determine if it was worth it or not. The worst-case scenario is that you, maybe, learned what not to do, or who not to use again in the future!

Remember, there is a reason why the best in the world use coaches. They help make them better by providing insight to what the athlete can't see and an outside perspective from someone on "your team" you can trust. Coaches enhance results. They are not required, unless you want to be world class or the best you can be. Then they are indispensable. You have to have one or more than one.

How Wise Do You Want to Be?

IQ, even as flawed as the test may be, is still one of the best predictors of success. But IQ is not the same as wisdom. We all have heard the story about the difference between "book smarts" and "street smarts." You should get both, but "street smarts" is better. Street smarts is more in line with wisdom than book smarts and IQ is.

The *Bible* teaches that wisdom is of more value than gold

and that you should sell everything to gain wisdom. With wisdom, you can always get more gold. But without wisdom, no amount of gold will be enough. For a fool and his money are soon separated (as I know all too well).

I was listening to a podcast with Tim Ferriss and Jamie Foxx, where Jamie was talking about how he became the success that he is. He immediately started talking about his grandmother who had nothing but an 8th grade education. But it was her life lessons, wisdom, and understanding that helped Jamie navigate the treacherous racist waters of his upbringing.

With a calm, talented and patient demeanor, Jamie was taught to let some things slide, pick your battles, and "cross the tracks" of life to make a positive impact. This woman may not have had a rocket scientist IQ, but the common-sense wisdom and street smarts was responsible for giving us one of the most talented and funny performers of our time.

Many of you may have known Jamie for his portrayal of Ray Charles. He was nominated for an academy award for that performance. But many of you may not have known Jamie for his portrayal of Wanda on *In Living Color*. *In Living Color* was basically a "black version of Saturday Night Live," only funnier. Jim Carrey also cut his teeth on that show with Fireman Jim and his version of a female body builder.

These early performances may not have been "Oscar worthy," but you have to start somewhere. From that 'somewhere,' you want to just keep working and improving your craft. When Jamie (and other performers) want to test out new material, they will go into many smaller venues and test their material. They may choose to launch a song on the East Coast. So they will hit every club they can and play their song. Or if they are a comedian, they will do as many smaller venues as the can to see which jokes "work" and which ones "bomb" based on audience feedback.

When I met Post Malone, he was just finishing a concert at a small venue in Grand Rapids called the Intersection. It was Easter Sunday, and I got the call to pick him up after the show. Post is a huge superstar now. But in 2015 he wasn't. He was a 20-year-old struggling artist, working his butt off to make his dream a reality. I mean, how many 20-year-olds do you know that would be working on Easter Sunday, away from friends and family to achieve their dream?

You might say, "Well, look at his success. I'd do that if I knew that was the result." The thing is, you don't know, and you won't. Neither did Post. He kept working anyway. Now he is known worldwide. And for the record, he was a really, good guy. Not only did he tip me $200, but the women he was with that night also confirmed that he was a real gentleman, never pressuring them to do something they didn't want to do. He even left me a compliment saying that "Robert is cool AF."

Not everybody likes Post and some have criticized him mercilessly, but he presses on, letting his success be the best revenge.

Tyler Perry on *Madea* is like that, too. Wise and very hard working. Hollywood said he couldn't do what he has done. He took their advice, and set it aside by saying, "I know the Hollywood way of doing things, and I think I will do it Madea's way." Look at him now.

Yes, street smarts and wisdom are much more valuable than a college degree and IQ. Get the degree, but don't rely on it. Rely on wisdom; it has a much better return. Unfortunately, wisdom is not being taught on college campuses these days. It's more political correctness and social nonsense that is doing more harm than good. Still, the degree is required in many companies and industries, so get the degree as inexpensively as possible (NO DEBT), and use it for what it is, a key on your key chain. It really is nothing more than that. A key that will open doors and possibly start an engine. Wisdom, on the other hand, is truly valuable.

"For the LORD gives wisdom; From His mouth come knowledge and understanding." Proverbs 2:6

How Much Mental Well-Being Do You Want to Enjoy?

How to treat others? I'm traveling on the "quiet car" on the train. A lady slams down her tray with a crash! Then she lets out a loud sigh and begins to work. The train hasn't left the station yet and I needed to make a quick call. I softly say into the phone, "Jim, I just got on the train, I'll be there in 2 hours," and hung up.

This lady basically shouts at me and says, "Excuse me, this is the quiet car!" Way louder than I was, waking up anybody who might be sleeping. I was pissed. Calm down, RJ, calm down. She's a cranky old lady and she is not going to control my attitude, so I quietly thanked her for reminding me and went back to work.

Then, later on, as the train was traveling down the tracks, I overhear a couple talking quietly, still on the "quiet car." Once again, the 'loud lady" shouts, "Excuse me, this is the quiet train!" Her obnoxious rebuke disrupted a lot more people than the original couple did.

Now, it was not right that they were talking. It was, in fact, the quiet train. But this lady was much more disruptive to the train than they were. How can people be so blind to their actions? Do they not know, or do they just not care? That's not for me to decide.

It appeared to me that she was an angry old lady and had allowed something outside of her control to "own" her thinking. Because she was owned by this thing outside herself, i.e. other people's behavior, she was angry, and she continuously tried to control the people around her even though they weren't under her authority.

No one is going to own my thinking without me letting them. I don't allow people to live in my mind rent free.

Gratitude: Serve Negativity and Pessimism Eviction Notices

When we let outside forces control us, we become resentful. And resentment is the root of bitterness. The flip side of resentment is gratitude. So if you want to kick out those Negative Nellies and Neds living in your head rent-free, practice being grateful for everything. Literally everything.

Gratitude is the world's most effective eviction notice to negativity.

Gratitude develops kindness and grace. Resentment, gratitude's opposite, develops bitterness and more resentment. Choose what you want, not on the minor distractions and annoyances, and then focus on the things that lead to what you want.

You know, caring about others is big part of being grateful. And it's a big part of how you can be grateful, peaceful, and content no matter what.

People pay attention to how much you care. They really don't care how much you know, how smart you are, or how much education you have (unless they are your doctor, attorney or accountant).

There was a story about a woman who attended two state dinners in Europe. On the first night she sat next to XYZ, and on the second night she sat next to PDQ. A reporter asked this woman, "What a great experience you had sitting next to two of the most prominent men in Europe. What was it like?" The woman replied, "On the first night I realized just how important XYZ was, and on the second night I realized just how important I was."

I tell the Post Malone story multiple times a day when I am driving. I show them the picture of the two of us and relay what a good man he is. It has nothing to do with his music either. It is more about who he is as a man. It is not a paid endorsement, just simply a good story to remind myself and others how important it is to treat other people.

The "marriage guru" Mort Fertel tells a parable, adapted from a story that has been attributed to Benjamin Franklin.

One day, Reuben bought an axe.

His brother, Simon, said, "Reuben, can I borrow your axe?"

Reuben said, "No" and refused his brother.

Then Levi, Reuben's other brother said, "Reuben, can I borrow your axe?"

But Reuben refused Levi, too.

Finally, Judah, the 3rd brother, came to Reuben and said,

"Reuben, I have always been good to you. Please lend me your axe."

But Reuben refused Judah as well.

Reuben's brothers saw how useful the axe was to Reuben, so they went out and bought their own axe.

One day Reuben was chopping a tree when his axe accidentally fell into the river. He searched, but he couldn't find it. His work wasn't done so he came to Simon and said, "I lost my axe and I didn't finish my work. Can I borrow your axe?"

Simon replied, "No! You didn't lend me your axe when I asked."

Reuben then approached Levi and said, "I lost my axe and I didn't finish my work. Can I borrow your axe?"

Levi replied, "When I asked to borrow your axe you refused me. But I'll be better than you. Yes, you can borrow my axe."

But Reuben was humiliated by Levi's reply, so he didn't borrow the axe. Instead, he approached Judah. Judah heard what happened and when he saw his brother coming, he said to him, "Reuben, I heard about your loss. Don't worry. You can borrow my axe."

Reuben hugged Judah and said, "Thank you for your kindness. But most of all, thank you for your forgiveness."

Be like Judah.

If you want to turn your relationships around, don't treat people the way they treat you; treat them the way you want them to treat you.

It's so easy to feel justified treating people the way they treat you. But then you'll be stuck in the same old relationship.

Of course, that raises giant questions: "How do I do that? How do I do that when I'm so angry? How do I do that when they're treating me so horribly? How do I do that when they've moved out? How do I do that when they're having an affair? How do I do that when they want nothing to do with me?"

It's not easy. But, again, it is only the secure that can be humble. Give thanks and do your best.

Psalm 138 says in times of trouble, give thanks.

Choose to be grateful. It is the antidote to envy. It is the eviction notice to resentment. It is the yeast in the bread of happiness.

Envy is deadly, look at Cain in the *Bible*. At its root, envy is felt to be so fundamentally bad because it highlights what is lacking and hates goodness itself.

Consciously, envy is painful because it is based in a feeling of deprivation. Ingratitude at its root not only robs you of joy, but literally can kill others. It kills marriages by seeing the supposed joy in other marriages. It kills your own mental well-being by constantly thinking about what you don't have and yes, it can even kill other people, as the brother Cain did to his brother Able when he became jealous of the relationship Able had with God. Yes, envy is deadly, so choose not to be envious.
But, how?

Drive envious "weed thoughts" out of your mind by overloading your own mind with the good, the pure, the honorable things around you.

The Apostle Paul teaches that if you want to have peace, then you need to focus (dwell) on the good first.

"Finally, brethren, whatever is true, whatever is honorable, whatever is right, whatever is pure, whatever is lovely, whatever is of good repute, if there is any excellence and is anything worthy of praise, dwell on these things. The things you have learned and received and heard and seen in me, practice these things, and the God of peace will be with you." Philippians 4:8-9

Now, you don't have to do that. You don't have to do anything at all, in fact. But if you want peace of mind and a good mental well-being, there is an answer. Choose to do it or choose not to. The choice is always yours and you will get what you choose.

If you still don't think you can do that, let me tell you another story from "behind the wheel" of my Uber.

This is a story about a heroin and crack addict. She said it was her daughter that saved her life, for once she had given birth to her daughter, she knew she had to stay clean. She went on to say that a coworker "Googled her," researched her and proceeded to print photos of her past when she was arrested and let others see the mugshots. She then passed along a rumor to the supervisor that she was still using and based on the rumor, they drug tested her.

The drug test, when it came back, was clean. She was mad at the coworker for violating her privacy, and equally upset with the supervisor for believing the rumor.

What amazed me about her was her attitude. She said, "I will kill them with kindness. I will forgive them. I will always have coworkers I don't like or a supervisor I don't care for. I will prevail."

Think about that for a second. Here is a drug addict, with a new baby, who is trying to turn her life around. Yet she has a coworker who is trying to sabotage her efforts. I'd be ticked off! She could have gone to the HR office and likely had this girl fired for what she did. But not her. She wasn't about to let someone else control her thoughts and actions. She was in control.

I told her, you forgive, you do right, and you keep working for you and for your daughter, not for them. That is why we forgive. Not for them, it is all for you.

The fact is she made my day.

Chapter Nine

Choose Who You Are and Who You Hang With

Who Are Your Friends?

Jim Rohn, my favorite motivational speaker, and mentor to Tony Robbins, famously said that you are an average of the five people you spend the most time with. The statement refers to the law of averages. It means, your circle of closest friends determines who you are, and what you want to be in life. The statement points out to the influence of people you hang out with.

You may not be able to choose your co-workers, or your family members, but you absolutely can control who you are friends with. Pay attention to your thoughts and actions when you are around certain people and then ask yourself this question:

"Is that ok?"

If you don't like the person you become when you are around certain people, stop hanging out with them. This can be subtle too. Nobody will allow someone to come up and shove them off course, but the subtle nudging that accumulates can take you far from your goals.

I remember talking with a young lady who had just gotten divorced. I asked what happened and she said that he was physically abusive and hit her. I asked her why she would date and marry a man that would do that to her. She said, "well he didn't start out that way."

Yes, he was sweet and kind and he romanced her early on and then one day, he disrespected her and she "let it slide." The small disrespect turned into emotional abuse, and then ultimately physical abuse. It was the slow, seemingly insignificant things that built over time that she refused to address immediately that doomed her.

My suggestion is at the first sign of disrespect or even unkindness, you address it immediately. You must be willing and able to tell someone to "go to hell" if you are going to have any power to negotiate. The problem is that once you become emotionally invested, and consider the time and effort put into a relationship it becomes harder and harder to say, "go to hell." That's why you do it early. Have your standards set up ahead of time for what you will and will not put up with. Remember, do not be deceived, what you allow, you approve, or as it says in the good book:

"Do not be deceived: "Bad company corrupts good morals." 1 Corinthians 15:33

Who Do You Love?

This crazy little word has gotten more people in trouble than anything else! Contrary to popular belief, you can choose who you love. Love has many definitions which is why it can get confusing. Just to name a few, there is a fatherly love for his children, a brotherly love for his friends, and then there is the erotic love he has for a woman.

You may be attracted to someone and have desire to be with them, but is that really love? Love is a verb. It is active and seeks the other person's best interest. You make sacrifices for the other person with no thought of what's in it for you. The greatest form of love is when you lay down your life for another person. There is no greater love than that.

Today love is not defined that way. Today love is a feeling, and it is all about what I want, and what I need. That is selfish, and that is not love. That kind of "love" seeks its own gratification and what will make ME feel good. That is what animals do. They act on what feels good and what they want, not what the other person wants and needs. Mature love is an act of the will and that means it is intentional and can be chosen.

I used to tell my children not to date anyone who you they wouldn't consider marrying. You might think that a bit archaic and extreme, but the reality is, once you start spending a lot of time with a person and developing a relationship, feelings may start to develop for that person and the next thing you know, you are in a relationship getting ready to walk down, the isle, simply, because you have invested so much time with them. Or worse yet, you end up like the girl from earlier in this chapter.

Have your principles and values set up ahead of time and know what your deal breakers are up front. Don't doubt me on this, there are a ton of people out there to date and/or marry. Be patient and know what you want. The feelings you have when you are first attracted to someone will fade and the cute little mannerisms that you find endearing will end up bugging you to death after a decade of time. So, check the emotions at the door and engage your brain. It is the single biggest relationship you will choose and will cause you great gain or great harm over time. Choose wisely.

What Should You Believe?

What you believe causes you to make decisions about your life. Good beliefs lead to good choices and ultimately good results, whereas bad beliefs lead to bad choices and bad results.

If you want some insight as to what you truly believe, take a look at your checkbook and your calendar. The two biggest assets you have are your time and your money. Where you choose to spend or invest them gives you a glimpse as to what you truly believe.

Build your beliefs around the truth, logic and reason. Pay attention to the results you get too. Your results are a reflection of your beliefs. Getting other people's perspective is also very valuable. You see, we all have blind spots, and other people can help us see things that we miss.

Where Will You Live?

One of the best pieces of advice I heard about where to live and work is to choose where you want to live and then find a job there. Too often we find a job and then allow the job to dictate where you live. This is a big beautiful world and there are some amazing places to live.

I presently live in Grand Rapids, MI. primarily, because that is where my ex-wife wanted to live to be closer to her friends and family. Then after the divorce, I chose to stay in Grand Rapids to be near my children until they graduated high school. Now, I can move anywhere in the world, but I still choose to stay here. Why? It's cloudy and cold in the winter, there aren't any really big mountains to climb or ski slopes to navigate. But, it's home for me. I like the culture, the people, the work ethic and the summers. It's tough to beat West Michigan in the summer time!

But I also love to snow ski and mountain climb. Denver or Salt Lake City come to mind when I think about those activities. Yet Denver traffic is a nightmare, and the Mormon culture in Salt Lake is a little different to say the least. The point is, you can live wherever you want to and where you choose to live will also affect your life in a real and profound way.

If you want some insight as to what you truly believe, take a look at your checkbook and your calendar.

Let's recap. You can decide:

1. Who your friends are
2. Who you love
3. What you believe
4. Where you live

Now here are some thoughts on what you can't decide.

Where Were You Born?

You can choose where you live, but you cannot choose where you were born. One of the common phrases I use when I meet people I borrowed from Dave Ramsey. When people ask me how I am, I say, "I am better than I deserve." Some people say, "Wow, what a great attitude, I think I'm going to start using that too." Others say, "Why are you so negative?" The last group says, "I don't know about that. What's so great?"

I go on to tell them that we are living in the greatest country in the world, and that we all have tremendous opportunities in front of us every day. Often times, they push back and say something like, "Well, I don't think this country is all that great."

I'll follow that up by asking them where they would rather

live? Which country has it better than we do? After all, 40 million illegal immigrants can't be wrong, can they?

How about Venezuela, or Russia or Afghanistan? Especially for a black female. No other country in the world is better for a black female than the USA. Everything is available!

Now, I'm not saying it's perfect, but it's about as good as it can get. What makes the USA great is the value that we place on the individual. Our constitution makes it clear that we get our freedoms from God and God alone. We are the only country in the history of the world to say that. Every other country is founded on the idea that government provides freedoms and rights. The USA sees the government as the vehicle to protect those rights that we have been inherently endowed by God the Creator.

Freedom of religion, freedom of speech, and the worth of the individual is paramount. The government is set up by the people, and for the people. The government is there to serve and protect, not hand out rights. Our rights and freedoms came from God, and God alone. That's what makes this such a unique and fabulous country.

You did not choose to be born here. It is a glorious privilege that millions of people around the world wish they had.

I think one of the best things for young people to do is to travel around the world. Especially if you do not think the USA is all that great. Go travel to China, India, or Africa. See what the rest of the world is like, and if you still don't think the USA is all that great, move! You are not a tree. You can choose to live wherever you want.

Who are Your Parents?

As much as we might like to change who are parents are, sorry, that one is not up to us! As the computer that created model Lisa in *Weird Science* said,

"They're oppressive, meddlesome, difficult, demanding, and totally bizarre. They're normal parents."

Yes, you may not think so, but your parents are normal. Not perfect, but normal, and perfect for you. Yes, even as oppressive as they are.

Whether you agree with them or not, no one will love you more than your parents will, ever. You may not think so, but they do want what is best for you. They have a different perspective, and they have years of experience on you and they love you and want what's best for you. Like it or not, they know you, often times, better than you know yourself.

They have seen you at your best and worst. They have changed countless diapers and know when you are moody, heartbroken, excited and depressed. They are not perfect, but their perspective is valuable to you. Listen to them. You don't always have to do what they say, but listen to what they are saying. There is value in there. Like it or not, there is value.

These idiotic parents will all of a sudden become like Albert Einstein when you get older, get married or have a baby. Overnight they seem to have become super geniuses.

What Period in History Were You Born?

Without a doubt, this has to be the best period in history to be alive, especially if you are in the United States, but really around the world. We live better than the Caesars of Rome lived. We have running hot and cold water. Food is plentiful, and major diseases have been mostly eradicated. In fact, most of the severe illnesses are self-inflicted. Things like heart disease, diabetes, and depression are all mostly a result of life choices.

Our technology is amazing. Our smart phones, things which didn't even exist in their present state until 2007. Rob Stothard/Getty didn't start using the term "smartphone" until 1995, but the first, true, smartphone actually made its debut three years earlier in 1992. It was called the Simon Personal Communicator, and it was created by IBM more than 15 years before Apple released the iPhone.

Now, with our smartphones we can navigate and communicate all around the globe. "Fake News" can be instantly researched and you can learn a new language, fix your car, and research whatever you desire, all with a few buttons.

The period of history called the "Dark Ages" was after the fall of Rome and civilization as the world knew it. The concept thus came to characterize the entire Middle Ages as a time of intellectual darkness between the fall of Rome and the Renaissance.

Enter Johannes Gensfleisch zur Laden zum Gutenberg, born in 1400. He was a blacksmith and goldsmith by trade. He also changed the course of history with his invention of the printing press. Through this single invention, the power of information distribution was taken out of the hands of the oppressive regime of the Church and placed in the hands of the people.

It was the access to information, books and in particular the *Bible* that led to the Enlightenment, the English Renaissance, the Reformation and the Scientific Revolution. No longer did we have to rely on priests to tell us what was in the *Bible*, we could now read it, interpret it and apply it for ourselves. This one thing—free access to information—is what transformed our world.

Today, the internet has the equivalent power that the printing press had in the 1400's. You don't even have to read, just pop open a YouTube or listen to a podcast of anything that interests you and you are on your way. And that small device in your hands, probably right now, your smartphone, gives you access to all of it.

Everything is available to us today. The only thing you need to supply is your creativity, discipline and execution. It is all available, and it is all up to you.

Today our access to information is not the problem. Where I see us lacking today is in our inability or neglect of discernment. We fail to filter the good from the bad so we do not know how to tell the difference between the truth and a lie. That is why a compass is needed--something to direct you to true north. We all need some rules to apply so that we can discern rightly.

Values and Principles — What are Your Rules for Life?

Your philosophy of life, the values you hold dear as well as your perspective will have more of an impact on your life than anything else. In the short book *Man's Search For Meaning,* author Victor Frankl tells about his horrific experience as a prisoner under Nazi rule. He was able to rise above his circumstances and maintain his mental clarity and attitude in the most terrible conditions. Now, I'm sure your situation is not as bad as his. There is no excuse. If he can do it, so can you.

It is a great book to read and it is not that long. It will change your perspective and change your life for the better.

A good thing to realize and be aware of is that there is good and evil in the world. Everybody has good and evil inside. Go looking for the gold not the dirt and draw that out.

Decide which dog you will feed. Here's what I mean. Sitting Bull once told a wise story that has been repeated down through the years. It might have been told to him by his elders, I imagine.

"Inside of me there are two dogs," he said. "One is mean and evil and the other is good and they fight each other all the time. When asked which one wins, I answer, the one I feed the most."

This story is similar to a Cherokee legend quoted in a blog post by Kuldip Singh. Singh writes the story of an old Cherokee grandfather who is teaching his grandson about life.

"A fight is going on inside me," he said to the boy. "It is a terrible fight and it is between two wolves. One is evil — he is anger, envy, sorrow, regret, greed, arrogance, self-pity, guilt, resentment, inferiority, lies, false pride, superiority, and ego."

He continued, "The other is good — he is joy, peace, love, hope, serenity, humility, kindness, benevolence, empathy, generosity, truth, compassion, and faith. The same fight is going on inside you — and inside every other person, too."

The grandson thought about it for a minute and then asked

his grandfather, "Which wolf will win?"

The old Cherokee simply replied, "The one I feed."

What Attitude Will You Choose?

What you focus on will be. King Solomon wrote in Proverbs 23:7 "For as he thinks within himself, so he is."

You will become what you think about most of the time. If you want more evil, ugly and bad, just keep watching the news, and look for it. You will find what you are looking for.

Jesus talked about knocking on doors, planting seeds and looking for things. You will find what you are looking for. The doors you knock on eventually will open and the seeds you plant will yield the proper crop. Pay attention to what you are feeding in your mind.

The story of Job in the *Bible* is about a godly and righteous dude. He made sacrifices every day, not only for himself, but also for his family. For Job said, "Perhaps my sons have sinned and cursed God in their hearts." Thus Job did continually.

He was a good man, but perhaps he was focused on evil just a little too much. He was concerned about what his children *might* have done. He wasn't thinking about the good they could be doing, no, he was focused on the bad they *might* be doing, and he made sacrifices accordingly for them.

Now, as the story unfolds, the Lord allowed calamity to strike Job. He lost his wealth, his health and his family. He then states, in Job 3:25, "For the thing which I greatly feared is come upon me, and that which I was afraid of is come unto me."

You see, Job was thinking, dwelling and greatly fearing calamity, and lo and behold, it came to pass.

When I was playing a lot of golf, visualization was a key aspect of the game. Especially as you get your swing down pat. I would stand over a tee shot and picture the arc of the shot as it exploded off my club slightly to the right of the fairway and gently draw the ball back into the middle of the fairway where it would come to rest perfectly.

Standing over a putt on the green, I would envision the ball's path and internalize the final second when it would drop with a "ker-plunk" in the cup.

It would never fail, on a water hole, when you were required to hit the ball over a body of water or place the shot on the green next to a river, when a golfer would stand on the tee and repeat to himself, "Don't hit it in the water, don't hit it in the water." You know where that ball was going? You guessed it, right into the water.

You see, the human mind doesn't understand the word "don't." So that golfer was telling his subconscious mind, "hit it in the water, hit it in the water."

What we think about will come to pass. Be careful of the seeds you plant, the plants you nurture for they will lead to the harvest you reap.

Of course, something awful was going to befall Job, that is what he was dwelling on his entire life. Remember, the dog you feed will win the fight.

Choose People over Things

Philip James Elliot (October 8, 1927 – January 8, 1956) was

an evangelical Christian who was one of five missionaries killed while participating in Operation Auca, an attempt to evangelize the Huaorani people of Ecuador. Jim was quoted as saying, "He is no fool who gives what he cannot keep, to gain that which he cannot lose."

I believe that people are more important than things. We use things to serve people, we don't use people to serve things. There is a divine spark in each of us that is God-like and as such, we should treat people accordingly.

But there is also evil in the world, and we can't be so trusting and naive that we allow evil to reign. That is why we must use good judgment and wisdom to know the difference.

Be Generous

Some people believe that there is a limited amount of money in the world, or they live with a scarcity mentality and if they don't take what they want, nothing will be left. Well, that's one way of looking at things. I believe that wealth can be created and that there is an unlimited supply because wealth can grow and build.

For example, take a pile of rubber, glass, and metal. There is a specific value in those raw materials. But, then get a few engineers together and they can turn that pile of raw materials into an automobile worth many times the original value of the raw materials.

There is no limit to the amount of wealth that can be created. It is only limited by our imagination, creativity and diligence. The more
 value you can create, the more wealth you will build.

There is a common word used today called "karma." The

word is often misused by Americans. It is a Hindu word that states that how you live in this life will affect you when you are reincarnated in the next life. But we generally mean "what goes around comes around" when we use the word. We use it as the idea of you reap what you sow. In this sense of the word, it is a concept found throughout the *Bible*:

"A man will be satisfied with good by the fruit of his words, And the deeds of a man's hands will return to him." Proverbs 12:14

"Knowing that whatever good thing each one does, this he will receive back from the Lord, whether slave or free." Ephesians 6:8

"If the righteous will be rewarded in the earth, How much more the wicked and the sinner!" Proverbs 11:31

I am reminded of an Uber story where a young lady wanted me to drive her to work every day for cash. Each week she would pay me $40 and I would drive her to work. One week she got behind on some bills and asked me if she could skip a week and pay me $80 the following week, to which I agreed. Sure enough, next week she paid me $80.

There is no limit to the amount of wealth that can be created. It is only limited by our imagination, creativity and diligence.

A few more weeks go by and once again she got behind and asked if she could pay me the following week. "Sure." I replied. But the next week she didn't pay. I told her that I don't do business this way and that I will have to cut her off unless she gets caught up. She promised that she was good for it and I said, "I know, but at some point, I will have to cut you off."

Sure enough, when the total got to $100, I told her she would have to find another ride until she could pay me. She said, "Robert, you know I'm good for it."

I said, "I know you are, but I don't do business this way. Just pay me when you can. I won't hound you for it either."

She said, "How do you know I just won't run off and never pay you?"

I said, "Because my girlfriend will never let that happen. In fact, you do not want to get on her bad side, she will mess you up. She's famous for it."

"You're crazy Robert, I don't even know your girlfriend," she retorted.

"Oh yes you do, she's famous," I said.

"What's her name?"

I said, "Karma."

She laughed and I didn't hear from her for 3-4 months. When she called in tears. She said, "Robert, what did you do to me? You cursed me, I tell you. You cursed me!"

"What are you talking about? I don't curse anybody. I just pray for them."

"Ever since I stopped paying you, I have lost my job, I lost my apartment and I've got nothing! I'm living out of my truck. You cursed me!"

"Now I told you I don't curse anybody, but remember, I said, you don't want to get on my girlfriend's bad side. She don't play!"

Sure enough, the next day another one of my regulars called me, and said they wanted to go to Chicago. Well, I didn't want to go to Chicago, but they said they would make it worth my while and pay me $300.

"OK," I said, "Let's go to Chicago." I still haven't received the money from Patricia, but I was paid another way. There are all sorts of ways to make money and God owns it all. He puts up one and puts down another, for He owns it all. As it is written in Psalm 50, verses 10-12:

For every beast of the forest is Mine, The cattle on a thousand hills. "I know every bird of the mountains, And everything that moves in the field is Mine. "If I were hungry I would not tell you, For the world is Mine, and all it contains.

One caveat, to whom much is given, much will be required. The more you have been given, the more accountable you will be. Be careful what you wish for.

Chapter Ten

How to Choose Freely

Decide to be Intentional

Be intentional about who you hang out with. Be intentional about which habits you develop. You are not a tree, you can move and change. Take action and be intentional with it. You are free to do whatever you want to.

You may be stuck in a crappy situation right now. Maybe you can't change your location right now. But you can change the direction in which you are going. Don't underestimate the small intentional changes that yield massive results down the road.

Just start. The only thing that goes with the flow are dead fish. Start swimming upstream, against the tide, and you will be unique.

Habits

Decide what habits you want. Habits are like this giant stone. The giant stone is your life, and what you believe. Why not what you do? Because your actions are a direct and inexorably connected function of what you believe. To change a habit, you must change an action and to change an action you must change beliefs.

Know your time and know your money, for those two give

insight to your beliefs.

Habits are like the rolling stone. It is already moving. That movement is called inertia and is the result of your past beliefs. Although you can change your beliefs right away it takes some time for the new action to become a new habit.

We like habits because it simplifies our decisions and saves energy. Good habits are harder to form but they are easier to live with than bad habits. You can change your beliefs and direction immediately but, the results will take some time.

Decisions take energy, thought and risk. Decide your habits and eliminate a lot of later decisions. For example, if you choose to create a habit of exercising the very first thing every morning, you don't have to decide that anymore.

Habits are malleable and can change and you, yes you have the power to change them, if you want to.

Rolling the Dice

Sometimes however, you really can't decide between two options. In those cases, just pick one. I heard of a guy that graduated college and had two excellent job offers. He was stumped about what to do. He honestly had no idea which one to take. So he wrote two letters. One was a letter of acceptance and the other, a letter of rejection. He randomly took the letters and put one in an envelope to one company, and the other in an envelope to the other. Then he mailed one of them, and opened up the letter he kept, to see what decision was made.

Sometimes the adventure of not deciding can be exhilarating. When I travelled for a month in Spain on the Camino de Santiago, I met random people and stayed in all sorts of random places. I had a major plan and goal of arriving in Santiago at a particular date, but other than that, I allowed the trail to come to me. I remained open to whatever experience happened to come my way. As a result, I met people from all over the world, and experienced a trip of a lifetime.

Things just happened to work out. Random acts of kindness were both given and received. This is truly a big beautiful world if you stay open to the possibilities.

How to Decide

Simply stated, take small amounts of time with small decisions and large amounts of time with large decision. The more important the decision, the more care and thought should go into it.

In his book *Blink* Malcom Gladwell reveals that great decision makers aren't those who process the most information or spend the most time deliberating, but those who have perfected the art of "thin-slicing"--filtering the *very few factors* that matter from an overwhelming number of variables.

The first knee jerk reaction is often times correct, if you have practiced the art of "knowing yourself." By knowing who you are, taking the item to ponder past decisions and how they worked you, you can begin to trust your "gut" more and more.

In high school they taught me that when I took a test I should stick with your first answer because it is often the correct one.

If you have ever been on a time share tour, you know that they are required by law to give you 72 hours before the contract is considered "good." This 'rising window' was put into place so people could take the time necessary to "cool off," and let the passion of the moment cool down. Things look differently after 72 hours, so make a decision, and then check it to see if it still 'feels' right.

Timing of Decisions

Sometimes it is best to put off a decision for a specific reason. When the Apostle Paul was falsely accused and thrown in jail, people wanted his head. They petitioned Felix, the governor, to take immediate action, but this is what he said:

But Felix, having a more exact knowledge about the Way, put them off, saying, "When Lysias the commander comes down, I will decide your case."

You will never know everything to make a decision, but once you have enough information, or time has run out, pull the trigger, make the decision and then make the decision right. But there are sometimes when you should be extra cautious when making decisions.

When Not to Decide-HALT

When you are hungry (H), angry (A), lonely (L), tired (T), stressed or under the influence of drugs or alcohol, those are not good times to make decisions. Some people will try and pressure you into making a decision right away. They can be intimidating and somewhat forceful or influential. Delay the decision and de-pressurize the situation by simply saying, "Thank you for your input."

When you have enough information. You don't need to know everything, but you need to know something.

When you are fatigued that is not a good time to make decisions. So eat right, exercise, etc.

Self-control is at the root of most poor decisions. When you are fatigued and hungry after a fight with your spouse is not the time to be making big decisions.

It's okay to delay, too. "Thank you for letting me know, I'll take that under advisement and get back with you."

Sometimes it's not. Knowing which decisions are important and immediate is helpful, but most decisions are not life or death and they can be postponed. Dating, investments, etc. They are like buses. If you miss one, just wait awhile and another will be coming around soon.

Others, however, are big. Be clear about what you want so when the opportunity presents itself, you can act. It's an awful feeling to realize the moment to strike has come and gone, leaving you to choke on the dust of regret.

Connecting the Head and the Heart

Should you follow your head or follow your heart? The wise thing or the passionate thing? The short answer is "yes." Those two do not have to be, or should they be mutually exclusive. Connect them both when making decisions.

One of the often-quoted verses in the *Bible* actually connects these two ideas in one simple verse.

Proverbs 3:5-7 "Trust in the LORD with all your *heart* and do not lean on your *own understanding*. In all your ways acknowledge Him, And He will make your paths straight.

Trust with your heart and don't lean on your own understanding. Notice however, it doesn't say, don't use your own understanding. Use your understanding, just don't lean on it. What should you lean on? The truth, your guiding principles, logic and reason. This is where
 your desires, goals and dreams come into play. Without exploring and acknowledging your desires you will end up like *Alice In Wonderland* again where it not only makes no difference what you decide, but you are likely to end up in a spot you never intended.

Number your days and solidify in your mind that you will die one day, and you need to align your desires, values and goals with that realization.

Mental Condition

There are some people out there scheming and trying to figure out ways to harm you or take advantage of your good nature. You can't be naive about the evil in the world. Most people are not evil, but there is a significant number to cause you to take notice. That is why you must "suit up for battle by putting on the full armor."

When the Apostle Paul was teaching the new Believers in Christ, he taught them to be aware of the schemes of evil by putting on the full armor of God.

Put on the full armor of God, so that you will be able to stand firm against the schemes of the devil. Ephesians 6:11

 The armor was of the Most High, and that included a helmet, shoes, breastplate, shield, and sword. Put it all on.

Calm and Clear: Hug the Cactus

When you are clear headed and at peace, decision making is more, sound, but when you are in pain, we find the idea of changing more appealing. It's the struggle that lets you fly, actually, it's the struggle that pushes you out of the nest so you can fly.

Pain is no fun at all. Physical pain, mental anguish, and feelings of loss hurt us. We avoid pain because pain sucks. Or does it? Of course, the sting of pain isn't pleasant, but the lessons learned through pain can be transformational.

What should you lean on? The truth, your guiding principles, logic and reason.

Instead of trying to run from, ignore or avoid pain, learn to lean into and feel all of the pain.

When I run long distances of 20 miles or more, I imagine I am getting ready to "face the dragon." It's the "wall", the beast within me telling me to stop, I can't handle it. That's when I try to lean in and play with the dragon and see just how much further I can go.

We go through all sorts of lengths to try and avoid pain. We distract ourselves with electronics and social media. Numb our feelings with alcohol and pills. Or lose ourselves' in the arms of another human being. These are all decisions that ultimately lead to more pain down the road.

Learn to lean in and take the pain. Feel it all and see where it leads.

One of the most painful experiences of my life was when my wife of 21 years wanted a divorce. I attended many groups of struggling divorced people and they all seemed to have a similar theme. The divorce wasn't their fault, or they wanted to justify their decision. I saw that as counterproductive.

Every relationship has two people involved so each has some degree of responsibility in the outcome. By shifting the blame entirely to the other person, you lose any opportunity to learn and grow for the next relationship. So, I took a different, more painful approach and simply asked, "If it was all my fault, what might have been the reason for her to divorce me?"

Let me tell you, that is not a fun experience! The last thing in the world I wanted to do was to honestly "look at me." Jonko Willink has a term for it called "extreme ownership" where he teaches that you own everything. Someone screws you over? Own it. An employee doesn't do their job? Own it. He is extreme!

The man who focuses on efforts and who stresses his downward authority, is a subordinate no matter how exalted his title and rank is. But the man who focuses on contribution and who takes responsibility for results, no matter how junior, is in the most literal sense, "top management."

But the reason is obvious. As soon as you decide to blame someone else for something, they are in charge and they own you. You become their slave. Not me! I own it all, it is all my responsibility. Nobody is going to own me.

The same is true with how you live your life. If you blame the USA, the patriarchy, rich white men, women, taxes, your family, your neighbors, etc. you no longer have any responsibility for the outcome. Better to say, "In spite of all of these perceived obstacles, I am in charge and I will take full responsibility and overcome." That is a powerful decision to make that will lead you to ultimate freedom.

Lean into the pain and own it all.

It's also more real and honest. I ran for State Representative in 2018. I lost. I took second place - first loser. I was crushed. It hurt and I was feeling really low. A friend of mine took me to lunch to try and cheer me up. I really appreciated him doing that. As a side note, true friends stick around in your losses and he stood by me. As the saying goes, success has many parents, but a failure is an orphan.

Anyway, he waxed eloquently about how Abraham Lincoln lost seven elections before he was a success and that I will overcome, etc. It was really very kind of him. But I stopped him and said, "TJ, it's too soon for that. Right now, I just want to feel the pain of the loss. I want to bathe in the negative experience and feel it all. I'll get over it, I know I will, but I want to feel it all right now."

Lost election, feel the pain, divorced, feel it all.

"Decide to lean in. Take the pain." *Platoon*

"He's not getting killed, he's getting angry." *Rocky 3*

When you hit the wall, keep running.

But my all-time favorite is "hug the cactus" with Robert Downey, Jr. and Mel Gibson.
https://youtu.be/_AAJuynxnTQ

Stop blaming and complaining. Hug the cactus. You do have what it takes, and you are stronger than you think you are. Lean in and let me show you how.

Mel Gibson was under scrutiny for some illegitimate comments he made in Hollywood. He couldn't get work and was "out" of the Hollywood scene. Then Robert Downey, Jr. came to his rescue one awards night.

You see, years earlier when Robert Downey, Jr was struggling with his own demons and couldn't get work, it was Mel Gibson who came alongside of him and gave him some work - and some advice. He said, "Instead of trying to avoid the pain and run from your demons, "Hug the cactus." Huh? Yes, grab hold of the cactus and hug it. Basically, he was saying to lean into the pain and feel it all. Be intentional and lean in.

Robert's career began to blossom and then took a meteoric launch with the massive success of the Avengers franchise. Robert was not just "back;" he overcame in a big, big, way.

Now, it was Mel Gibson's time 'on the edge.' At the award ceremony in October 2011, while receiving an award, Robert Downey Jr. took the attention off of himself, and turned it to Mel Gibson, telling the story of how Mel helped him in his time of need when no one else would. Robert then said, "He's hugged the cactus long enough," and he hugged Mel. Man, that was great.

Leaning in and feeling the pain isn't about being a masochist or a glutton for punishment, it's about being real, being honest and being human.

I had another painful experience right out of college when I was working at the Fifth Third Bank in Indianapolis. I wanted to be a husband and father and businessman, have grandchildren and great-grandchildren in my life. Yet instead of pursuing things that would lead in that direction, I was partying like a rock star and not pursuing things that would lead to the end I wanted. After the bank robbery, things changed in my head, and I decided to stop doing some things and started doing others.

I had a successful t-shirt business in college and stopped it because "it was the thing to do."

So I took a full time, life-draining banking job that was like death by a thousand little cuts every day. I hated it.

We generally will not make a decision until it is forced upon us. Why does it take a heart attack to get into shape? Why does it take a financial catastrophe to start working on your financial plan? Why does it take a divorce to really look inside of yourself to see the type of person you are?

Diet Strategy

One of the keys to a successful diet is to have a plan or a strategy throughout the day. Have a meal packed when you leave the house so when you get hungry, you have something easy to grab. The WORST time to make a diet decision is when you are STARVING and see the Golden Arches coming up over the hill. The WORST time to grocery shopping is when you are STARVING.

Gambling

The time to worry is before you place the bet, not after you spin the wheel. The place to decide about what when and where to gamble is BEFORE you leave for the casino.

Drinking

If you think you might be drinking, take an Uber downtown and leave your car at home. Eliminate the temptation of saying to yourself, "I'm ok to drive." If you don't have your car, there is no risk of driving under the influence.

Emotional State

The heart wants what the mind believes, and our eyes are the window to our soul.

Make decisions when emotions are cool.

Set things out the day before.

Give your keys to someone else. Decision made, no brainer.

Turn off your phone.

Once a Couple Has Sex, People Get Stupid

I was driving a young lady one morning and she was telling me the story about how her relationship with her man was not going the way she had hoped. I simply stated, "Well, once you have sex your brain stops functioning properly."

I might as well have hit her upside the head with a tennis shoe. The look on her face was one of clarity, and yet she was simultaneously dumbfounded. "Oh my gosh. You are so right."

There is something that happens when you are intimate with another human being. Sex is more than just a physical act, it connects your soul and spirit to another person and as soon as you engage in that, your mind changes and you cease to think clearly about the relationship. It has a higher degree of importance and commitment making it much harder to make decisions.

That is why I say don't date anyone who would not be your mate. If you honestly can't see yourself marrying them, don't date them. Don't waste your time and open yourself up to problems. I would much rather have you spend a few less years with the right person than a few more years with the wrong one.

Chapter Eleven

Make a Choice and Check the Results

Know When to Cut Bait

Knowing when to throw in the towel, and move on, can be tricky. If you have been honest with yourself, and sought feedback, and not run from outcomes, you may have trained your "gut" in such a way that you can trust it. It can be tough to know if you are "throwing good money after bad" or "just one more round of financing" to get you to where you need to be. Just be as honest as you can with yourself and remember that the more you invest in one area, means you cannot invest in another.

Sunk Cost vs Opportunity Cost

A sunk cost is the money that is already invested into a project. It's gone. Opportunity cost is the loss of one opportunity by investing in another. For example, if you invest $10,000 in one venture, that means you can't invest $10,000 in something else. That "cost" is the lost opportunity of what you could have invested in.

The same holds true for dating. If you are dating one person, you can't date another. The more time you spend with one person, that is the sunk cost of investing in that relationship. Sex is a massive "sunk cost" and investment. When sunk costs get really big, it becomes harder and harder to walk away from them.

It's Time to Re-Create Your Movie

Decide what you want your life to look like, just like a screenwriter and director would create a movie. Because that is exactly what you are doing. If you don't like certain characters in your movie, write them out in the next scene or change the role that they play. If you don't like the location of the set, move. You are the screen writer, and director, as well as the actor in your own movie. That movie is your life.

One of my favorite scenes is from the movie *The Holiday* starring Jack Black, Jude Law and Kate Winslet. The little old guy told Kate Winslet that she is a leading lady, but she is behaving like the best friend. You are supposed to act like the lead in your own story.

Decide what you want, ask what you need to do to get it, and then go do it. You'll make mistakes for sure, but they will be your mistakes and you will learn from them and grow. You will regret the things you never try more than the things you try and fail at. Go for it!

Remember, sometimes things that look good aren't and things that appear bad are actually good. In the movie *Charlie Wilson's War* there's a story about the lucky kid.

Toward the end of *Charlie Wilson's War*, a CIA officer, played by the pitch-perfect Philip Seymour Hoffman, cautions the Wilson character (played by Tom Hanks) not to be too sure they have done something glorious. To make the point, he tells the story of a Zen master who observes the people of his village celebrating a young boy's new horse as a wonderful gift. "We'll see," the Zen master says. When the boy falls off the horse and breaks a leg, everyone says the horse is a curse.

"We'll see," says the master. Then war breaks out, the boy cannot be conscripted because of his injury, and everyone now says the horse was a fortunate gift. "We'll see," the master says again.

You see, you never know exactly how things will play out. You never know what the tide will bring in tomorrow, and if you just be patient, and let things marinate, you could have a tasty treat. Just keep your head about you, and know that other than death, nothing is permanent.

"Success is not final, failure is not fatal: it is the courage to continue that counts." Winston Churchill

Now, all of the following things are bad, awful experiences that I would never wish on anyone. I am not candy coating them, they suck! However, by taking these bad things and using them they best way possible can transform your life.

It was like when Joseph's brothers sold him into slavery. Joseph didn't say it was a good thing, he said it was bad. But he went on to say, "that which you wanted for bad, God used for good."

My being held hostage in a bank robbery forced me to take a fresh look at my life and re-evaluate what I was doing. It got me married, earned me an MBA and gave four beautiful children.

My marriage and ultimate divorce is another success-and failure-in my life. I would not travel around the world, write all of these books, run for political office and impact all of the people I have with Uber had I stayed married.

"We will see."

Give it time.

"Difficulties strengthen the mind, as labor does the body." Seneca

There are always two ultimate outcomes. Win or lose. Good or bad. But there is also a middle part where you got some good and some bad, which is frankly the way it really is. Instead of win-lose, think win-learn.

Henry Ford said, "Whether you think you can or you can't, you're right."

Learn by your own experience or by others'. That's why paying attention is so important. Street smarts. Experience is a thorough and brutal teacher. Best to learn some things from others' experience. Which is why books are so important. You can anything you want.

Gutenberg transformed the world with the printing press because people learned to read and opened their minds - and their whole world - to new ideas. Yet today nobody reads. Now we have audiobooks, YouTube and the internet. It's change, yes, but it's not loss. It's Gutenberg on steroids!

We have so many choices! Not only of what to buy, where to live, what to do.

Henry Ford is also famous for saying, "You can have any color you want as long as its black."

Back in the day, there were no choices like we have today, and we have the ability to be aware of all the choices on our $1M smartphones. Yes, I know they don't cost $1M, but there is over $1M in technology available at your fingertips.

There used to be a standard agreed-upon set of beliefs. What you heard from your parents (who stayed married, by the way) was the same thing your teacher at school taught you that aligned with the preacher on Sunday.

Shoot, just ten years ago there were only two genders. A boy with an XY chromosome or a girl with an XX chromosome.

There is now literally an infinite number of choices available to us, making the decision-making process infinitely more complex as well as uncertain.

As I look back on the decisions I've made in my life, there were huge decisions I had to make that turned out didn't matter all that much. Then there were others that I thought were insignificant that changed the course of my life.

In twenty years if I am still alive, I'm sure it will be the same when I look back on today.

You may be thinking, "So nothing matters. The good offsets bad, it will all work out in the end?"

Well, yes, in some ways...but a resounding "no!" in other ways.

As I travel across the country for work, I see homeless on the street. Once busy streets in south Chicago are scattered with only a few people due to gun violence. The idea that 'nothing matters' just because we can't be sure about our decisions doesn't make any sense on these streets.

Tell a mother or father that just lost their son to a random drive-by shooting it doesn't matter. Tell that to the baby with brain damage because his mother wouldn't stop drinking.

I heard about a mom who took morning sickness drugs, given to her legally prescribed by a doctor. What nobody knew at the time was those drugs caused severe birth defects. Horrible right? Of course it is. Nobody would wish that on a mother and child. Yet, it was exactly because of that horrible event that we have had many life-affirming changes in our country for people with disabilities, including the Americans with Disabilities Education Act.

It can be argued that the daughter made it happen. The good that she did as a result of her physical limitations transformed our nation's landscape, helping other disabled people, veterans etc., in the process.

Once viewed as freaks and relegated to their homes, immobile, ostracized and dependent, she removed barriers to living a full life in society. In doing so, she gave them and key that offered them freedom, independence, and a whole new world.

Who Gets to Decide?

In the film *Bull Durham,* Annie said, "Well, actually, nobody on this planet ever really chooses each other. I mean, it's all a question of quantum physics, molecular attraction, and timing. Why, there are laws we don't understand that bring us together and tear us apart."

Crash Davis replied, "After 12 years in the minor leagues, I don't try out. Besides, uh, I don't believe in quantum physics when it comes to matters of the heart."

Or in the musical *Guys and Dolls,* Sara waxed eloquently about how to choose a man worth marrying. "Sky Masterson" replied, "No, no, no. You can't do it like that. What are you picking a guy or a horse?"

"I wouldn't expect a gambler to understand."

Sky said, "Mine I'll leave to chance and chemistry."

"Chemistry?" she asked, intrigued.

"Yeah, chemistry," he replied with a devilish grin.

Do you have control, or are we all circumstances of fate? That question has been pondered since the dawn of time. As discussed earlier in chapter 4, the answer is "yes" to both.

Today there continues a debate about who is better equipped to choose and make decisions for our lives. Some believe that individuals are too dumb and stupid and cannot be left up to their own devices so the government has to decide what is best. They believe that all power, money, and control belongs' with the state, and the state will determine what is best for us.

Then on the opposite of the debate is the individual who thinks the government is corrupt and should never be put in charge of any decision of a human being. Money, power and control belong squarely in the hands of the individual, and the state should only have a very limited say in what we do.

I contend that the worth and value of the individual takes priority. Every single one of us has a spark of the divine within us, and to sacrifice that gift by relinquishing control to the government is poor stewardship. Obviously, there are those who cannot take care of themselves, and they need some kind of assistance, but that should never encroach on our own individual rights and liberties.

At the end of the day, the person best equipped to make the decision should make the decision. Who knows the situation the best, who knows the players in the game being played, who understands the desired outcome, etc. ...that's the person who should decide.

Let's look at a few common scenarios to get the idea.

Parent or Child?

When a child is born, he is completely dependent on the choices of the parents. But, as the child grows up, the wise parent begins to give more and more control to the child so they can grow and develop into independent members of society. There is always going to be a battle between the young and the old, parent vs child. That's natural and normal. Nevertheless, at some point the parent needs to let go and not only allow, but push the child to make their own decisions. Otherwise, they will live in the parent's basement until they are 50!

In Janet Jackson's song "Control," she sings:

When I was 17, I did what people told me
Did what my father said,
and let my mother mold me
But that was a long ago,
I'm in Control - Never gonna stop
Control - To get what I want
Control - I like to have a lot
Control - Now I'm all grown up

Boss or Employee?

The boss may have ultimate responsibility for a decision, but a wise boss also understands that often times, the front-line employee knows better about what needs to happen. The military is the same. Of course, the ranking officer is in control, but the man on the front line has real time immediate feedback about how the battle is being waged.

In *Start-up Nation: The Story of Israel's Economic Miracle*, a 2009 book by Dan Senor and Saul Singer about the economy of Israel, they discuss how the culture of Israel encourages push back and challenges the status quo. So much in fact that privates in the army will often challenge superior officers. They encourage this to perfect their decision making and to be circumspect in their understanding. They realize that with a "top-down" command and control system, you are limited by insight and perspectives, but when others challenge with open debate, a better decision is often times achieved.

> *Instead of win-lose, think win-learn.*

Have a structure in place, but also be open to feedback that doesn't line up with your perspective, it just may lead to a better outcome.

The person best suited to the job is the one who has the responsibility to decide.

So how do you decide who is best suited? Ask yourself these questions...

Who has the Expertise?

If you are ill, see a doctor. If you have a legal issue, see an attorney. Need your taxes done, see your CPA. Building a house, hire an architect. Sure, you can probably study and figure all of those things out on your own, and believe me, being your own advocate is important. Don't blindly follow a person's advice. Learn as much as you can and then ask questions, stay engaged in the process and understand what is going on.

Who is Responsible for the Result?

As much as you can, put decision makers on the same side as you. Make the outcome you are looking for contingent on the persons advice or decision. For example, when I was in charge of Operations for a Manufacturing company, I instituted a productivity plan that put management and employees on the same page. If goals were met, then both parties would enjoy the benefits.

Management was encouraged to clear away roadblocks so production could produce. At the end of the day, if the goals were met, each party reaped the benefits. If they didn't, they didn't. It was no longer about who was at fault, it was more about, what has to happen to get the job done, and they worked together as a team to make it happen.

Who Has My Best Interest at Heart?

Parents

Like it or not, generally your parents have your best interest at heart. You don't have to like or agree with what they say, but no one will love you more or knows you better than your parents do. They want to protect you from their mistakes and the pain they experienced in life. They are coming from a perspective that is different than yours, and they may be way off base with their thinking, but understand, it is coming from a position of love and concern for you. They truly do want you to succeed.

Senior Citizens

Older people have such a unique perspective. They have lived much longer than you and their lack of political correctness and tact can be refreshing. They will say racist things, make chauvinistic comments, and generally tell you the truth, from their perspective. Listen to them, you will gain a wealth of information.

Whoever has experience in what I want.

If you want to be wealthy, listen to wealthy people. If you want a great marriage, listen to couples that have been married 50+ years. Healthy, healthy people.

Don't get wealth advice from a broke person, or marriage advice from a guy that's been divorced three time.

As the old saying goes, "Success leaves clues."

Where to Decide?

Before you can make another choice, you need to choose where you will make your decision. It's the choice before the choice.

I was told years ago that a good diet begins in the grocery store. I was also told, don't go shopping when you are hungry. "No brainer," or "I have no choice in the matter," or "It is beyond my control."

When you know you will be in an emotional, or feelings-based environment, make the decision ahead of time. For example, write out the check you will give, prior to showing up at the fundraiser.

Give your keys to someone else if you know you will be

drinking or better yet, just take an Uber to begin with and remove the temptation.

In Homer's *Odyssey*, Odysseus had the crew of his ship actually tie him to the mast before he sailed in front of the sirens on the beach. He also instructed them to put wax in their ears so they would not fall prey to their temptations. That is an example of making worse decisions, and understanding the risks ahead of time, and then removing all options.

Burning your boats is also an example of this. Once the boats are burned, there is no other option other than to win, or die.

How to Decide?

Know yourself and be honest. If you're broke, say "I'm broke!" There is a big push today about affirmations and manifestation. The theory goes something like 'just affirm what you want, and you can manifest it into being.' Part of that I agree with, you do need to visualize what you want, and you do need to internalize it and make it a part of you. That is a good thing.

But you also have to work. If you're fat, say, "I'm fat." If you're broke, say "I'm broke." You have to deal with reality and then visualize what you want, take action and hold yourself accountable.

The "Getting Things Done" guru David Allen has many tricks and shortcuts for getting things done. But, one thing he struggles with is packing for a trip. He knows that about himself and plans accordingly. David sets a time limit and doesn't start packing until 40 minutes prior to leaving his home. He knows he can pack in 40 minutes. If he gives himself more time, he will take it and it won't make the decision any better. It's just a waste of time. He doesn't try to change who he is, he sets the plan around his own style, and who he is.

Plato, Socrates, Seneca and other great philosophers that focus on logic, reason and critical thought also say, "Know thyself."

Not All Decisions are Created Equal

You may be familiar with the 80/20 rule or the Pareto Principle. The Pareto Principle (also known as the 80/20 rule, the law of the vital few, or the principle of factor sparsity) states that, for many events, roughly 80% of the effects come from 20% of the causes.

But, Ben Gay III and Mark Harris taught me about the 151-rule. If you follow 80/20 idea a little farther, you will see that 1 decision can account for roughly 51% of the results.

Follow me if you will.

20% is responsible for 80%

So that means 20% of 20% or 4% is responsible for 80% of 80% or 64%.

Take it one step farther and you see that 20% of 4% is roughly 1% (.064) is responsible for 80% of 64% or 51%.

That means that 1 decision is responsible for 51% of the outcome.

Not all decisions are created equal. The key is to find the 1% that is the fulcrum to the other 51.

I have a friend that had a very rough upbringing. He was

raised in the south side of Chicago and street life was just part of growing up. There were guns, violence, drugs. Fathers were scarce, and so, young boys were left to their own devices to survive and live. The life expectancy was not much more than 25 for these young men in the hood.

My friend made a decision one day to turn his life around. He found the Lord, cleaned up his act and started to work in legitimate jobs and stop dealing drugs. He learned how to be a supervisor and manage a crew, but he wanted more. He came to me with an idea for a non-emergency transportation business. He just needed some money to buy a vehicle and put his business plan into action.

> *At the end of the day, the person best equipped to make the decision should make the decision.*

The bottom line is that he now has a successful enterprise with over 17 vehicles servicing West Michigan. He still has to overcome racism, and hurdles that are only seen by a black man. He has to constantly keep his mind clean, and clear to make sound decisions, and not let the racism get the better of him.

Often times, it's easier to get out of the hood than to get the hood out of you. Rich Flowers story. Yes, he is oppressed. Racism yes. Yet he chooses every day to overcome that.

He sees clearly what is going on and deals with the truth of the situation in a wise manner. The person who ignores, obfuscates or denies the truth will always be at a disadvantage to the person who holds the truth in high regard. The highest regard. Falsehood leads to false beliefs, false hope and bad results. Failure. Like building a house on the sand.

Beliefs and values are the roots or the foundation. If you don't like the fruit, look at the roots.

Beliefs

Decide what beliefs you want to control you. Just like your habits can and will change, so do beliefs. Should you use your beliefs or the truth when making decisions? Ideally, they should be consistent.

Beliefs vs. Truth

My son asked me one morning what's more important belief or truth. The reality is, they should be the same. Belief, or more accurately, correct belief or mature belief is based in truth. Immature, or foolish belief, separates truth from belief.

I don't care how much faith, or belief I have in my abilities, I will never play in the NBA. And that's okay, because no matter how good or how strong King James is, he will never be a professional jockey at the Kentucky Derby.

Good belief is based on truth, bad belief is based in lies.

The problem lies with how faith or belief has been defined and changed over the years. In the *Bible,* faith is described as logic and reason applied to the truth. The world seems to define belief as something separated from the truth, which is just foolish.

Children believe in Santa Claus because they are children and parents tricked them into thinking it was true. As soon as we got older, we put away those foolish ideas and started to use logic, reason, testimony from others and evidence to refine our thinking and act accordingly.

As Paul said in the *Bible* "When I was a child, I used to speak like a child, think like a child, reason like a child; when I became a man, I did away with childish things." 1 Corinthians 13:11

As you grow, mature, win, lose and have new experiences, you gain perspective and insight. This, in turn, causes you to see the things you see as "true." All this means is that your beliefs change. But beliefs, regardless of what happens to us or what we 'think,' should always be based in the truth.

Truth

One of the most important things to consider about our thoughts is, "Are they true?"
Too often our thoughts are just not true. We need to focus on what is authentic, real, and lines up with God's Word.

One caveat to mention here. Experience is recommended in all areas except sexuality. Decisions, like habits and beliefs, affect one another. You've decided evolution and climate change are real or true. Your filter is now altered to line up with that programming and you will act accordingly.

Evolution, the disproven theory, describes man as nothing more than a chance happening that through countless mutations became you and me. From goo to you by way of the zoo. So to speak. This faulty idea debases and depreciates the human being thereby encouraging an even more cynical, temporary and existential existence. No wonder depression, anxiety, and suicide are so prevalent today.

The Power of One

These catalysts or "keystone habits" as Charles Duhigg

relays in his book *Power of Habit* can have a profound impact on results. Alcoa's CEO Paul O'Neil, when he took over in 1987 addressed the investment community with an unorthodox approach. He said, "I want to talk to you about worker safety."

The room went silent.

"Every year, numerous Alcoa workers are injured so badly that they miss a day of work," O'Neil continued. "Our safety record is better than the general American workforce, especially considering that our employees work with metals that are 1500 degrees and machines that can rip a man's arm off. But it's not good enough. I intend to make Alcoa the safest company in America. I intend to go for zero injuries."

The audience was bewildered. Hands went up asking about inventories, profit margins and cash flow. To which O'Neil replied, "I'm not certain you heard me. If you want to understand how Alcoa is doing, you need to look at our workplace safety figures."

For the new CEO, safety trumped profits.

Or did they? Are those two mutually exclusive or mutually reinforcing? You see, over Paul O'Neil's tenure as CEO, Alcoa's profits quintupled. That's a 5x improvement for the primary measurement of a CEO. But, not once did he focus on profit, rather he focused on workplace safety.

One of the most important things to consider about our thoughts is, "Are they true?"

This "keystone habit" had a ripple effect throughout the

organization that impacted how Alcoa worked, how the planned and ultimately how they performed, resulting in a massive improvement in profit, not to mention an employee injury rate that dropped from 1.86 lost work days per 100 workers to 0.2. By 2012, the rate had fallen to 0.125.

There are many so-called "keystone habits" that have a similar effect on your life, your relationships and your business.

Here are some keystone habits to consider:

Saving 10% of your income.
30 minutes of exercise each day.
Reading 30 minutes each day.
Eating an apple, a day.
Being generous every day.

Take exercise for example. The simple act of exercising not only helps your physical body and how it functions, including digestion, heart rate, blood flow, etc. It also has a profound impact on your mental state, and well-being. The increased blood flow to your brain and extremities is powerful, but so is the feeling of accomplishment and knowing that you did something positive. I have found that one little 30-minute block of time invested, actually helps me be even more productive the remaining 23 ½ hours each day, allowing me to get even more done than when I don't exercise.

Saving 10% and having a budget does similar things to my life. When I save 10% and work off of a written budget, I feel like I got a raise because the habit of being intentional with my money actually makes it go farther by not allowing many leaks in my financial boat.

Test your own keystone habits to see what works best for

you. Often it is not the 12 extra things you need to do that makes the difference, but the one habit consistently repeated every day that makes the difference in many areas of your life.

Goals: It's About the Journey *and* the Destination

Have a goal and take aim at a target. The Apostle Paul teaches this idea when he said,
"Therefore, I run in such a way, as not without aim; I box in such a way, as not beating the air." 1 Corinthians 9:26

Decision making is dependent upon a goal, a target or an aim. Without a goal to shoot for, decisions really don't matter. So the first thing when making decisions is to have a goal, a target and desire. That will guide your decision-making process. Some basics on goal setting, make them big and make them long term and make them yours.

Remember *Alice in Wonderland* from earlier? Without a destination in mind, it doesn't really matter. It is kind of like the captain of a ship that won't decide on a direction in which to go. It doesn't really matter where he goes, so he goes with the flow of the ocean, and wherever the current takes him.

A Caveat about Goals

Goals are powerful. Goals are motivating. Goals are good for limiting options and for providing clarity in decision making. Basically, goals are great for getting from chaos to order, but creating order in your life is not the end game. Order is simply a stepping-stone for developing creativity to becoming a patriarch in life.

Goals can get tricky once you try to move from order to creativity. Why? Because goals work. They encourage intense focus and fuel desire. The problem is that they block out everything else and dial you in. When you're in chaos, that's exactly what you need, but once you've mastered chaos and achieved order, creativity is the goal of a patriarch. That demands knowing when to shift gears and not be as orderly or as focused on a particular target. If you are so focused on a particular goal, you will sacrifice the creative portion that is required for patriarchy.

Here is a story from Jordan Peterson's workshop on essay writing:

However, you should let it (the rules) guide you, until you know better. You have very little right to break the rules, until you have mastered them.

Here's a little story to illustrate that idea, taken in part from a document called the *Codex Bezae*.

Christ is walking down the road on the Sabbath, when good Jews of that time were not supposed to work. In the ditch, he sees a shepherd, trying to rescue a sheep from a hole that it has fallen into. It is very hot and, clearly, the sheep will not be in very good shape if it spends a whole day in the desert sun. On the other hand, it is the Sabbath. Christ looks at the shepherd and says, "Man, if indeed thou knowest what thou doest, thou art blessed: but if thou knowest not, thou art cursed, and a transgressor of the law." Then he walks on down the road.

The point is this: There is a rest day for a reason. Otherwise people would work all the time. Then they would be chronically unhappy and exhausted. They would compete each other to

Without a goal to shoot for, decisions really don't matter.

death. So, if it's time for everybody to rest, then rest, and don't be breaking the rule. However, it is also not good to let a sheep die in the hot sun, when a few minutes of labor might save it.

So, if you are respectful of the rule, and conscious of its importance, and realize that it serves as a bulwark against the chaos of the unknown, and you still decide to break it, carefully, because the particularities of the circumstances demand it – well, then, more power to you. If you are just a careless, ignorant, antisocial narcissist instead, however, then look out. You break a rule at your peril, whether you know it or not.

Rules are there for a reason. You are only allowed to break them if you are a master. If you're not a master, don't confuse your ignorance with creativity or style.

Rules, goals and targets are there for a reason, to help the naive become wise and to create order out of chaos. But, once you have mastered the art of order, you have earned the right to break the rules so you can become a master patriarch

Apply Logic and Reason to Evidence

These are complicated times for us. It seems as though everything that was nailed down has been undone, and what we thought was common sense, is no longer so. In fact, common sense is not all that common anymore.

What is common sense? The obviousness around us and our wisdom applied to it. Today the political-correct police have stifled free speech, and even the suggestion of something as basic as someone being a boy or a girl comes under fierce attack.

My suggestion is let the social justice warriors do their thing, and you focus on the truth, and reality of the way things actually are. I was talking with one of my daughters and I told her that if she is walking down the sidewalk and sees a sketchy looking dude coming her way, I suggest that you go to the other side of the street. She objected by saying, "Dad, that's judgmental and profiling!"

"You're darn right it is!" Don't be an idiot. There are evil people in the world and God gave you a brain to use and wisdom to apply. Use it."

You see, I could care less about appearing judgmental or offending someone when it comes to the safety of my daughter. Sorry, she comes first, not some politically motivated social justice nonsense. Use your head.

Understand the Way Things Actually Are

There is the way you want things to be, the way you can change them, and then there is the way things
actually are. Wisdom deals with the way things actually are. Wisdom uses the way things actually are, and applies logic, and reason to them with critical thought.

Wisdom understands that there are exceptions to rules, but wisdom works on the rules first before looking at exceptions. The 80/20 comes into play again here. Most of the time, things are a certain way. Wisdom starts there and then adjusts accordingly. A fool bases his life on exceptions and ignores the obvious. Living in a fantasy land of his own creation.

That's fine, it's a free country. Think and live the way you want. Just don't make me pay for your mistakes and foolish thinking.

Time on Earth is Finite

We all have the same end-result, and we all have the same purpose. We all will die, and we all are preparing for eternity. We will all be dead a lot longer than we will be alive. Our purpose is to use the finite and limited time that we have, to prepare for the ultimate end-result. After all, you will be dead a whole lot longer than you will be alive.

What is Its Nature?

In the movie *Silence of the Lambs,* Hannibal Lector, played by Anthony Hopkins, was trying to teach Clarice, played by Jody Foster, how to get into the mind of a serial killer by asking, "What is its nature?"

She stumbled around, offering all sorts of FBI taught lessons of power, violence, and the like.

In response, Hannibal curtly shut her off by saying, "No! That is purely incidental. He covets."

The nature of the killer was he covets. He desires something he doesn't have. That is its nature. Once you know its nature, then you can know how to catch him.

Ask yourself, What's its nature or where's the kernel of truth?

Try to get to the bottom of the issue or decision. Look for the kernel of truth, by asking, "What is its nature?"

There is the way you want things to be, the way you can change them, and then there is the way things actually are.

If you want to have a blockbuster movie, what is the key issue? The story, special effects or location? No, hit movies are based on Star Power. People go see movies for the movie stars. Starring whom, that is the key issue.

You want to be in the movies? Take all the acting classes you want, but the key issue is, "Who is your agent?"

Getting to the heart of a decision can be a challenge. King Solomon had this issue come up when a case was brought before him to decide.

Two women each claimed a newborn infant was hers. How would you decide between the two? Would you listen to compelling testimony from each? Would the emotional expressions of each sway your discernment? Maybe gather witnesses to help?

You know what Solomon did? He called in a guard and told him to cut the baby in two and give ½ to each woman. Wait, what?! That's right, he ordered the baby be cut in two!

You may think that cruel, but what other way could he decide between the two? How could he know which woman was telling the truth without making that order?

But what you may not realize is, that ordering that action, Solomon was able to get to the heart of the issue. You see, once the order was given, each woman acted very differently. The lying woman said, "OK, go ahead and kill the baby." But the real mom deferred and told the king that the other woman could have the baby.

This told Solomon all he needed to know and gave the baby to the mother, who was willing to release him to the other, instead of the one that was willing to let it die.

Sometimes, it takes a new way of asking or approaching a problem to get to the heart of the issue. We are emotional creatures and that emotion often clouds our judgement.

One trick I use to minimize the emotional part of a decision is to ask, "What would you advise your son to do?" This removes much of the emotion but still maintains the care and concern for the outcome.

Another thing I do is to ask my "older self" what I should do. Imagine yourself twenty years from now. Looking back, what would you tell yourself to do?

Life Doesn't Really Matter...Simultaneously, Nothing Matters More than Life

If I were to ask you who Steve Jobs was, or Jeff Bezos or Warren Buffet and Donald Trump, you could tell me immediately. And, If I asked you who Thomas Edison was, Henry Ford and John D Rockefeller, you would likely be able to tell me. What about Stephen Girard, Nathan Mayer Rothschild and John Jacob Astor?

Any ideas?

Those last three were the richest men in America in the early 1800's. Even though virtually everyone knew who they were back then, nobody knows who they are today.

What's my point? In time, nobody will remember you and what you did. Our life isn't really all that important. That is, until you discover your personal meaning and purpose for being here.

Life is full of difficulties and suffering, nothing is going to change that. Maybe, just maybe, we can have a purpose and meaning in life that makes the suffering worthwhile. That is what Victor Frankl did in *Man's Search for Meaning*.

"To believe in God is to see that life has meaning." Ludwig Wittgenstein

Maybe trying to minimize our own suffering by making wise decisions makes sense, or maybe helping minimize someone else's suffering makes it all worthwhile. I think so. At least, that's how I choose to live my life.

Give someone a cool sip of water in their desert of life. Pick up some trash to make our environment just a little bit better. Offer a stranger a kind word. It may not change the world, but it might just change their life and yours, too.

We Want What Others Have (Envy)

Desire is a good thing, envy is bad. Desire is simply wanting something, envy on the other hand is desiring something that belongs to someone else. That's bad.

It is how we get what we want that is important. For example, if I want $1 million, I can go about getting it through stealing and taking improper advantage of others. Or, I can go about getting the $1 million in the service of others. The desire for the $1 million isn't the problem, it is how you go about acquiring it.

We think we are better than we are (vanity) or I'm at least better than you!

"All is vanity and striving after the wind." King Solomon reflected upon pondering his life. He spent his life in the pursuit of wisdom, and getting to the basic nature of life, and our time here on earth. He concluded that all is vanity and striving after the wind. At the end he said this, "To eat, to drink and to enjoy oneself in all one's labor in which he toils under the sun during the few years of his life which God has given him; for this is his reward."

He continues, "Enjoy life with the woman whom you love all the days of your fleeting life which He has given you under the sun, for this is your reward in life and in your toil in which you have labored under the sun."

We think we are worse than we are (self-critical).

I see this mindset more with women than men, although it occurs in both. I remember when I was married and we were getting ready to go out for the evening. She would get out of the shower, do her hair, apply the makeup, put on a sharp outfit, fancy shoes, nice jewelry and immediately look in the mirror and say,

"I don't like my hair, my makeup isn't right, I need new clothes, new jewelry and shoes." Then she would top it all off by saying, "And I need to lose 10 pounds."

Now, me on the other hand, I'd get out of the shower, run some gel through my hair, look in the mirror and say, "Dang! I'm looking good!"

Now, the reality is, I probably wasn't as critical as I should have been, and she was overly critical. The fact is, we are skewed in our perceptions and we should be aware of that, and not be so hard, or so easy on ourselves.

We are Afraid

We are fragile people. We are vulnerable to violence and being taken advantage of. We don't like feeling weak or fragile, but we are. Most of what we do is an attempt to mitigate this reality and create an environment where we can feel safe for some time.

We Want to be Liked

Human nature is a powerful thing and we are hard wired to fit into the group. Likeability is a key component to how and why we do things.

There is Good and Bad

Good takes you where you want to go, bad takes you farther away.

You can and will change (or at least you should).

"As a result, we are no longer to be children, tossed here and there by waves, and carried about by every wind of doctrine, by the trickery of men, by craftiness in deceitful scheming." Ephesians☐

Use Your Imagination And Emotion To Your Advantage

Worry is often a result of the negative use of imagination. These emotions paralyze you and keep you from doing something or making a decision.
Hope is the opposite. Hope uses imagination and emotion to illicit a positive action in the present.

Clarity and organization clear the decks for good decision-making while disorganization or chaos leads to impulse.

Make A Plan

Once you have a goal in mind, write it down and start to

make a simple plan for accomplishing it. You don't need all of the information, just a general idea is good enough to start. Remember, once you start down the path and make decisions toward your goal, things will change. You will become more aware, and wise, you will have additional information made available to you, and you will see things differently than when you started.

"It's not the plan that's important, it's the planning." Dr. Graeme Edwards

"A good plan today is better than a perfect plan tomorrow." George S. Patton

That's why you don't have to have all of the details to start. Just start moving toward the goal, keep score, and adjust accordingly as needed. Early detection, early correction. Don't get bogged down in the details. *Planning* pays off before you take action, while you are taking action, and after you have taken action. The most obvious benefit of *planning* is that it helps you anticipate possible contingencies, so you can avoid avoidable problems and take advantage of advantageous opportunities. But the operative word here is ACTION. You have to take action and execute to make the plans a reality.

Or, as Peter Drucker said, "Plans are only good intentions, unless they immediately degenerate into hard work."

Break Big Things Into Little Things (Next Action Idea)

It just takes a little nudge to get going. In the book *Nudge: Improving Decisions about Health, Wealth, and Happiness* written by University of Chicago economist Richard H. Thaler and Harvard Law School Professor Cass R. Sunstein, first published in 2008. Basically, just get going. It only takes a spark to get a fire going. A jump into the pool. A phone call. Just one small thing.

The 2-minute drill is great for this. Set your timer for two minutes and start a project. You only have to go for two minutes. At the end of two minutes, reevaluate. Often times, it is the simple act of starting an unpleasant task that is all that is needed to keep me going.

Hope uses imagination and emotion to illicit a positive action in the present.

Don't underestimate these small actions either. A simple 1% improvement compounds!

Just a 1% improvement repeated each day has a compound effect. Small consistent effort is key.

Mathematically, it can be expressed this way: Each day, repeated without any improvement will yield the same result in one year (365 days).

$$(1.00)^{365} = 1.00$$
$$(1.01)^{365} = 37.7$$

Doing nothing at all
Vs.
Small consistent effort

$(1.00)^{365} = 1.00$

Each day, repeated with a 1% improvement will yield

massive results in one year (365 days)

$(1.01)^{365} = 37.7$

Chapter Twelve

Tools For Decision Making

These are the four primary attitudes you need to make good decisions:

Good Judgment
Truth
Desire
Good Faith (as opposed to bad, immature or stupid faith)

Now, with these in mind, these are the 12 indispensable tools for making the best decision every time:

Ben Franklin's T-chart. List the positives on one side and the negatives on the other.

Let God or Fate decide. Remember the guy earlier who couldn't decide? He wrote two letters and then he blindly picked one and mailed it.

"David went out to meet them, and said to them, "If you come peacefully to me to help me, my heart shall be united with you; but if to betray me to my adversaries, since there is no wrong in my hands, may the God of our fathers look on it and decide." 1 Chronicles 12:17

Have a fleece. Gideon was told by God that he would defeat the Midianites with only 300 men. Gideon was not certain he understood God correctly so he asked if he could have a sign. He set out a fleece of wool and asked that God make one side wet from dew in the morning to reassure Gideon that he understood God correctly and sure enough God did, so Gideon went out to battle and defeated the Midianites.

You might have a fleece by saying, I will ask my closest friends and family their honest decision about a girl I am dating and if one of them says anything negative, I will break up with her.

Roll the dice. Similar to blindly mailing letters, rolling the dice removes all of your preconceived notions about a decision. Not sure who should get what? Roll the dice and let the dice decide.

"And they crucified Him, and divided up His garments among themselves, casting lots for them to decide what each man should take." Mark 15:24

"The cast lot puts an end to strife and decides between the mighty ones." Proverbs 18:18

Get counsel. The money you pay for experts can be the cheapest investment you make, provided you take their advice. Professionals are unemotional and have the wisdom and experience to help you make wise decisions.

Friends, although they may know us the best, tend to screw it up because we pick people who support what we want and support our preconceived notions. They screw it up by telling you what to hear.

Break the decision up. Let one person cut the pie and let the other person choose which piece to take first. This is a great way to get children to understand fairness!

Play the third party. We tend to give better advice than we follow. What would you tell your best friend or your child?

What would you tell your son to do? And the corollary, "Never trust a decision you don't want your mom or dad to know about."

By putting a decision in this context, you remove much of the emotion in the decision while maintaining the care for the outcome.

Decide quickly, change slowly. But, change if needed. Is difficulty a test or a tragedy?

Set a timer or make a time limit to gather the information you can and then make the decision.

Football teams score an inordinate amount of points in the final two-minutes of each half. They put in place their 2-minute offense where they have a specific goal of scoring in a limited amount of time (2-minutes). You can do the same by setting a timer, and starting a project, or making a decision.

Let the wise help you decide. Friends, experts, and parents. Yes, parents. For most of us, our parents are the ones that love us the most. No one has our best interests at heart more than they do. And remember, the older you get, the smarter they'll get.

So if you're young and your parents are still the subject of much eye-rolling, try to tune into your future self and take them seriously. Even if it doesn't make sense right now, ask for their counsel and take it to heart.

Good friends with morals, values, and steadfast character are also great to turn to in times of decision.

"I say this to your shame. Is it so, that there is not among you one wise man who will be able to decide between his brethren." 1 Corinthians 6:5

"Though you have felt through all my goods, what have you found of all your household goods? Set it here before my kinsmen and your kinsmen, that they may decide between us two." Genesis 31:37

Make the small decision first. Don't decide to get married on the spot. Start with a phone call, then a lunch date. Decide and test or check the results. Immediate short, medium and long term. Accountability and Time.

Once you make decision, give yourself some time and then review how it went. This review and recalibration will not only help you course correct, or reinforce the decision you made, but the review process will help you make better decisions in the future.

What are you becoming or what will you become? Know what the outcome is, or what it should be. Many young people mistakenly believe that the test for a good job is what they are making per hour. At the start of your career, your hourly wage is probably one of the least important things. Instead of asking what you are making per hour, ask yourself, "what am I becoming?" A solid company name and good longevity with them will have a bigger impact of opening doors in the future. Don't step over dollars to pick up nickels.

What have others done who chose that path? Wouldn't it be nice to have a crystal ball to see the future? Well, we do have something close to a crystal ball, old people and others that have done what you want to. Look at what they do, ask them questions, then put into action what you've learned.

This is a great short cut to getting to where you want to go.

Your spirit. How are you sleeping?

You can have all of the right information, make the wise decision and still you don't feel right about it. Take a gut check. No not are you taking probiotics. What does your gut say? This is where practice, review, experience, paying attention and discernment comes in. IF a decision isn't letting you sleep well at night, double check your findings talk it out with trusted people and if it still isn't right, change it.

I had a property I was looking at buying. The numbers made sense, it was within my local area to manage and fit all of my criteria but, it would mean I would have to foreclose on a family and kick them out their home. It was perfectly legal, they were severely behind in their taxes, and the court had even mandated that they leave. But they were still there. To get occupancy of the home, I would have to get the Sheriff involved and have them remove the tenants. I didn't feel right about it, so I didn't move forward. There are other deals to look at and invest in, this just wasn't going to be one of them.

This leads me to my next idea, principles.

Your guiding principles. Ray Dalio's book *Principles* is a textbook on decision-making and the principles behind them. I highly recommend it.

Some of my guiding principles are people, which are more important than things.

No fool is he who gives what he can. Never keep to gain something, that he can never lose. Pay It Forward, or the Magnificent Obsession principle of anonymous giving.

Make a bet and challenge yourself. This book is a direct result of a challenge I made with Tony Rubleski of the Mind Capture Group. We were both talking about new book ideas that we each had, so I challenged him to a 30-day plan.

We each would write and produce our books for review to each other.

Now, could this book have been better had I given it a 12 month or longer time frame? Maybe, but there is also a strong possibility that it would still be sitting in my mind with nothing being produced. Something done is better than perfect unfinished.

Know where you are and be honest about it. Knowing yourself is important. Know your prejudices, your likes dislikes, desires etc. Write them down in a journal and consistently get your thoughts on paper. Then review them often. Take an hour at the end of the week to see what happened. Take a half day at the end of the month and take a weekend or longer at the end of the quarter. Spend a week unplugging and review your year. What went well, what didn't, take the time to be like a good football coach or player and review the tapes.

Understand the times and know what to do.

"Of the sons of Issachar, men who understood the times, with knowledge of what Israel should do, their chiefs were two hundred; and all their kinsmen were at their command." 1 Chronicles 12:32

Managing the downside is more important than the upside. Protect your downside and the upside will take care of itself. Wealthy people understand that minimizing losses is much more important than maximizing your gains. A 10% loss requires an 11% gain just to get back to even.

Ask yourself, "What is the wise thing to do?" "Against stupidity even the gods are helpless."

Ask yourself, "What is the wise thing to do?" Not, "What would Jesus do?" You're not Jesus and if you want to bring Him into it, a better question might be, "What did Jesus and His disciples 'teach' in The *Bible*?"

Remember, wisdom understands the way things are most of the time. Then wisdom applies logic, reason, and critical thinking to the equation. The wise man lives in reality; fools live in fantasy land.

My favorite place to learn about wisdom and wise thoughts is in the book of Proverbs in the *Bible*. It is 31 chapters long and it takes only 5 minutes each day to read a chapter. In only one month, you will have started the understanding of Solomon's wisdom!

Some of you may be thinking, "Why only one chapter a day? Why not read it all in one 30-minute session?" Well, you can but, there is something both refreshing, cleansing and nurturing by doing a little every day. First of all, you start developing a new habit. Second, you start the day with something wise, positive, and encouraging. Finally, it is like setting the sail for the daily journey.

Or, more simply, you take a shower every day, right? You don't take 365 showers at once do you? Why not? The same idea applies here. You get dirty every day, and you need to clean your body, and your mind, and your spirit every day, too.

5 Whys. Ask 'why' 5 times to help get to the root of an issue.

SWOT analysis. Review the Strengths, Weaknesses, Opportunities and Threats of a decision.

Tools For Making Decisions Stick

Decisions are like willpower. They take energy, and we have a limited supply of energy, so use it wisely and only on decisions that really matter.

Wisdom understands the way things are.

A good way to conserve the energy of decision making is to create habits that require no more decision making or willpower.

Malcom Gladwell in his book *Tipping Point* introduces an idea that it takes 10,000 hours to become proficient or an expert at something. 10,000 hours is the equivalent of 5 years of 40 hours each week, after which point, you become an expert. You may take 2 ½ years of 80 hours, but 10,000 is the magic number.

It has been said that it takes 21 days for a new habit to form. So, somewhere between 21 days and 5 years, there is a desert of effort where you work and work and work and may not see the results you are looking for.

That's why coaches, accountability partners, and friends come in handy. Humans are tricky creatures and we like to be efficient in our time, doing the bare minimum to get the result we want. But there are no shortcuts with a new skill or talent, the work must be put in. So, we use confrontation, competition, and challenges to motivate and sustain our effort. This is what tests prepare for us. We intentionally set up football games, invite people to watch the performance, and we keep score, so we know how we are doing.

It helps us to "carry our cross," pick up a load (our responsibilities), put a stake in the ground and press on. It all starts with a decision to do, be or have something.

RunBet

RunBet is a program that allows you to put up money to encourage you to run. You decide the amount to bet, and you decide the amount to run. Then, at the end of the program, everyone who completed the task they agreed to, splits the pot.

Test and Go Small

Borrowing money on an idea will magnify it. I'm not suggesting that you borrow money to start a business, but know that money magnifies decisions.

When I was a stockbroker, some managers would encourage the new hires to go out and borrow as much money as they could to buy a fancy car, or big new house and pile up mountains of debt. The manager knew that once a broker had a huge mortgage, that alone would motivate the young salesperson to go out and sell, sell, sell.

Likewise, if you have a new business idea and borrow a lot of money to make it happen, that will magnify your decision, and immediately make it bigger than it was. It's one thing to use your personal vehicle to drive with Uber, but it's quite another to borrow money and buy a fleet of cars or trucks and get into the transportation and logistics business.

New business ventures have a very high failure rate, so it is often best to start small, test the idea, and the market, and grow organically. That will minimize stress and allow for better decision making in the future.

> *For new ideas and decisions, test and go small.*

Make the decision, then make the decision right.

KISS

Keep it simple stupid. Complexity is the enemy of execution.

Marriage

A force multiplier or a steroid. Create & Multiply the good or create and multiply the bad. Probably the single biggest, most impactful decision you will ever make.

Chapter Thirteen

The End is the Beginning

You have many of the same qualities as an animal. Desires, appetites, need oxygen, food, etc., At the same time, what we have that they don't have is a conscience and ability to choose. Making intentional and conscious decisions outside of our base instincts is one thing that separates us from the animals. In other words, using our imagination, coupled with desire and making decisions is what makes us uniquely human. Animals rely on instinct, as humans we have the freedom to choose.

Free Will or Fate?

The short answer is, "yes." Both are 100% true. You do have 100% free will, and fate will 100% determine your outcome. Wait, what, how does that work? I don't know, but it does.

It's one of those things that you just have to accept. If you ever think you are in 100% total control, just remind yourself of things that you weren't in control of, and whenever you feel like you have no control, remind yourself that you do.

Act as if you have 100% control and pray as if you have none whatsoever.

Minority Report

Trust in counsel but, trust in God's word above all. Why?

Well, for one thing, thousands of years of people have been using it and it has stood the test of time. No other book has been printed more or studied more and tested more. There is truth as well as valuable principles and insight in there. You can try and recreate the wheel, but a clever short cut, or a wise short cut might be to just use what people have already tested and tried for generations.

Moses had just led the people of Israel out of slavery from the Egyptians. After all sorts of miracles were performed in Egypt, God topped them all by causing the Red Sea to part miraculously and drown all of the Egyptian soldiers who were in hot pursuit.

Then the people were faced with a decision. The Promised Land was in front of them, but it was inhabited with giants and the people were afraid. God promised them the land if they would just go in and take it.

So, Moses sent ten spies into the land to check it out. Eight of the ten spies came back and reported that the land was good. It was a land flowing with milk and honey, but there were indeed giants there and the Israelites would be like grasshoppers among them. These eight advised against going into the land.

But, the other two spies came back, and they too said that the land was good. It was flowing with milk and honey and yes, there were giants there, and they were big. They continued, our God is bigger. If He promised the land to us, we should go in and do what He said to do.

Well, in one of the classic mistakes in leadership, Moses sided with the majority and did not go into the land. I didn't have to tell you, but God was ticked off and not happy with Moses. After all that God had done to prove His faithfulness and power to them, now, in their finest hour, they act like sheep and retreat in fear.

God said, "None of you over 40 years old will ever go into the promised land, except for the two spies who were faithful to Me. Joshua and Caleb, they will go in, but none of you will. And that is what led to Israel wandering around the desert for 40 years."

The moral of the story is, get good counsel, but trust in the Lord, and above all his Word.

Control Your Spirit

"Like a city that is broken into and without walls Is a man who has no control over his spirit." Proverbs 25:28 NASB

Integrity Focus And Action

It is time to rediscover and reclaim your mission. Simon Sinek, in his 2009 book, *"Start With Why"*, says that we all have a message or a purpose that is uniquely ours and that it doesn't change. That purpose or message is your "Why" and it doesn't change over time. Tap into your "Why" and connect it with the world you are a part of.

"He who has a why to live for can bear almost any how."

— Friedrich Nietzsche

Look around you. The world, your country, your state, your city, your neighborhood, and your family need you. There are lots of hurting people out there suffering and you're the one to do it. Find your mission and then live it. Your decision to play small isn't doing anybody any good.

Decide which dog you're going to feed. Then feed the one you want to win the fight. It's still a fight. How do you feed the dogs in your head? With your intention, attention, and with your habits.

Resolve means I will persist until. I climb mountains, run trails and marathons to test myself and strengthen my resolution muscle. I'm harder on myself than anybody. I took the hardest classes, the most challenging teachers and put myself through the paces to prepare myself., for bankruptcy, divorce, death, suicide, jail and even being taken hostage at gunpoint in a bank robbery.

"I'd rather attempt to do something great and fail than attempt to do nothing and succeed." - Robert H. Schuller

Your Days are Limited

In Psalm 90, Moses prayed to God that "He would teach us to number our days, that we may present to You a heart of wisdom." How does God teach us that? Maybe through a near death experience. Mine was through being held hostage at gunpoint in a bank robbery at 23 years old. I had others through losing friends to suicide and automobile accidents, family members that died. At funerals we come face to face with our own mortality. Life is a precious gift that we have been loaned from God. We will return it someday at which point He will ask, "How'd you do?"

Talk news radio play-by-play analyst, Rush Limbaugh often says that he has "Talent on loan from God. It will be recalled someday." He's exactly right. We all have talent on loan from God, we all have that divine spark within us.

King Solomon has a Poetic way to think about life and death. He calls it a "silver cord," a "golden bowl" and a "pitcher by the well."

"Remember Him before the silver cord is broken and the golden bowl is crushed, the pitcher by the well is shattered and the wheel at the cistern is crushed;

Nobody likes to be rejected. Making decisions is risky. You risk being made a fool, being rejected or worse, but rejection is better than regret. As author and reporter Sidney J Harris says, "Regret for the things we did can be tempered by time. It is regret for the things we didn't do that are inconsolable."

The difficult path is usually the best, at the least it is less crowded. So, stay hungry, stay unsure and live the adventure. Robert Frost's famous poem about two roads diverged in a wood comes to mind. It was the lesser worn path he chose that made all the difference.

Sure, you will likely fail along the path, you will even appear to be a fool at times. Scars are painful to earn, and yet they build character and always remember that scars are proof that you are stronger than whatever tried to kill you.

To enjoy life is to enjoy the process, and gratitude changes everything. This may sound like pollyannaish nonsense, but it's true. Some of my happiest days have been spent entirely in my own company, eating, lifting, and doing whatever suits me. Be grateful for the fact that you're able-bodied, young, and male. Be grateful for the fact that you have the opportunity to improve yourself physically, mentally, spiritually and socially. Be grateful for the fact that you can bring value, service and laughter into other people's lives.
It is amazing how simple acts of kindness can change a person's life and it doesn't take all that much either. Life really isn't all that serious.

You won't know until you try. Blessing in disguise? Remember the story from the Zen Master earlier? Success at first leads to failure later. Failure at the outset leads to success. Just work hard, be wise, fear God, take responsibility and enjoy life. After all, much of life is out of your hands anyway, so be the best you can be, and be faithful to opportunities.

"For I have taken all this to my heart and explain it that righteous men, wise men, and their deeds are in the hand of God. Man does not know whether it will be love or hatred; anything awaits him." Ecclesiastes 9:1 NASB

"Rejoice, young man, during your childhood, and let your heart be pleasant during the days of young manhood. And follow the impulses of your heart and the desires of your eyes. Yet know that God will bring you to judgment for all these things." Ecclesiastes 11:9 NASB

Stephen Covey in his *7 Habits* book encourages the decision to move from the URGENT and NOT IMPORTANT, to the NOT URGENT and IMPORTANT. NOT IMPORTANT things shouldn't be done at all, and important things should be decided in a NOT URGENT state of mind.

I add my own spin by shifting my focus from the temporal to the eternal. Work on things that last forever, not on things that pass away.

I gave an Uber passenger a $100 tip one time, yes, I was the driver not the passenger mind you. It made me feel great. I'll remember that forever. What is the value of that gesture to her? $100 and maybe a spark of a new belief in the goodness of man? Who knows, maybe she just thought I was a guilt-ridden white man. It doesn't really matter. I gave the money for what it did for me, not what it did for her. Maybe it helped her, maybe it didn't. Maybe it kept her lights on that month, maybe she shot drugs through her veins.

What was my value? How do you put a price on helping another human being?

Consider Oscar Schindler in the film *Schindler's List*. What was the value of his generosity? It became an obsession to Oscar. He just wanted to keep giving and giving and giving until finally his accountant told him, "It is enough."

Choose what you become addicted to. The early Christians did this by addicting themselves to the ministry. You choose your habits or addictions and then they choose you. You can choose them, the choice is yours. You are not a tree, you can move, and you can change.

"I beseech you, brethren, (ye know the house of Stephanas, that it is the first fruits of Achaia, and that they have addicted themselves to the ministry of the saints."
1 Corinthians 16:15

Walter Idema, one of the original founders of the Steelcase Company, had an obsession. He learned about this obsession from the Lloyd C Douglass book, *The Magnificent Obsession* written in 1929. The theme of the book is based on a passage from the Gospel of Matthew (chapter 6:1-4):

"Take heed that ye do not your alms before men, to be seen of them: otherwise ye have no reward of your Father which is in heaven.....That thine alms may be in secret: and thy Father which seeth in secret himself shall reward thee openly."

The philosophy behind the book is also partly that of "pay it forward", the idea that good deeds received are not to be paid back to the doer of the deed, but to a needing person in the future.

Giving anonymously became an obsession of Walt's and is one of the reasons why Grand Rapids is known as the second most philanthropic city in the USA. In case you're wondering, Provo, Utah is number one.

Walt's philosophy was carried on by others in West Michigan with the Amway founders, DeVos and Van Andel, Meijer family, the Bissell's, etc.

You might not be able to help at the level of these families, but you can help someone and in ways they never can.

Remember, sometimes the best help is not to help at all and let them struggle on their own to figure it out.

The Caterpillar Story

A caterpillar stuffs himself on a juicy leaf and the dreams of becoming more than he is. He drifts to sleep and a cocoon forms around him that protect him while the transformation takes place. The cocoon turns into a chrysalis and then he begins to struggle to get out. The struggle is fierce and difficult, and eventually a little wing pops out, then another, until finally the beautiful butterfly flies away.

Scientists have studied this miraculous process and have shown that if you were to cut open the chrysalis just a little bit to make it easier for the butterfly to emerge, he will never be able to fly. It is the struggle that developed the wing strength that allows him to fly.

Sometimes helping someone is not in their best interest. In fact, it can have the exact opposite effect you intended.

It all goes back to wisdom, values, truth, and judgment. That's why I believe it takes both a mom and a dad to effectively raise a child.

That's why older people that have lived a good life should be watched and listened to.

What's the worst thing that could happen? You might lose money or time. You might be humbled or humiliated. Yet you will have lived fully.

When you are guilty of something, never underestimate the power of your ability to abandon truth and reality. We will do just about anything and believe anything to justify what we do and clear our conscience.

How do you clear a conscience and address your own guilt? Admit it was wrong, ask forgiveness and make it right to the best of your ability.

That is just another reason why the God of the *Bible* and your relationship with Him is so important. It helps deal with our shortcomings as well as the guilt that goes along with it.

Goals are, or should be connected to your "why." Simon Sinek does a good job of articulating this as does "begin with the end in mind" by Steve Covey.

For a thorough and very personal approach use Jordan Peterson's "future authoring program."

Decide what you want from people. You both play a part.

A story…

A man once came to a town and asked the local sage, "I'm thinking about moving here. What kinds of people live here?"

The sage asked the man, "What kinds of people live where you came from?"

"Where I'm from the people are liars, cheaters, and mean spirited," the man responded.

"The people are the same here," said the sage.

Then another man came to same town and asked the same sage the same question, "I'm thinking about moving here. What kinds of people live here?"

The sage asked the man, "What kinds of people live where you came from?"

"Where I'm from the people are wonderful, kind, and courteous," the man responded.

"The people are the same here," said the sage.

People are as they are. That's true. But they also are as we are.

What do you get when you smile at someone? Usually a smile back. And if you stare at someone? A stare back.

We do not see our hand in what happens, so we call certain events melancholy accidents . . .
Stanley Cavell

Stop Blaming and Own It All

Divorce is a great example of this. I can't begin to count the number of people who say their husband/wife was a narcissist, emotionally abusive, etc. When asked, why would they marry such a person, without fail they say, "well, they weren't that way when I married them." To which I reply, "What did you do to change them?"

Never underestimate our ability to justify our own crap!

In my experience, every time someone accuses their spouse of being a narcissist, the accuser is a people-pleasing conflict-avoiding passive personality who lacks self-esteem. In other words, the dysfunctional dynamic between them was the result of dual responsibility. But it is so much easier to just blame someone else for your problems, then you have an excuse and never have to change.

It is like a child sitting in a poopy diaper. It may smell bad and needs to be changed, be he likes it because it's warm and it's his!

Get clear about what you want or at least what you think you want. Let me repeat "what you want." You don't really know, and it will change. It doesn't matter, just get clear. Start with basics. Mind, body, spirit, money, work, family, etc.

Pay attention to what you are doing, keep score, stay accountable to what you're doing, how it's working, and adjust if needed. Pay attention to others feedback, advice, mentors, etc. keep moving and keep refining.

Keep the critics guessing by constantly moving and employ the "corkscrew landing" approach to achieving your goals. A corkscrew landing (also spiral landing) is a method of landing an aircraft that is intended to minimize the risk of the aircraft being hit by anti-aircraft fire from the ground on its way to a destination airport.

Instead of slow descent towards the airport, in a corkscrew landing the aircraft is positioned at high altitude above the airport, then descends rapidly in a spiral. The maneuver is typically performed by pilots of military aircraft to avoid surface-to-air missiles. Or, in our case, dodging criticism. The pilot stays laser focused on his target approach (goals) and the circles the area, refining his course the closer and closer he gets to landing.

Sometimes the goal is foggy. You have a general idea, but not exactly sure. Just start working in that direction and as you move the object will become clearer. It can take some work to refine your goals. It's a little like those magic eye pictures. Remember those posters that didn't look like anything until you stared long enough, and the picture magically appeared?

Like helping you discover what was there all along. Then when you discover it. Viola! Or eureka! "I've discovered it!"

> "We shall not cease from exploration
> And the end of all our exploring
> Will be to arrive where we started
> And know the place for the first time."
> T.S. Elliot from *The Little Gidding.*

Get experience to help you develop ideas and discover more about yourself. Travel, explore, read books. Decide to do something challenging, worthwhile and exciting. When the goals are higher the risks are too.

Much of what I stumbled into by following my curiosity or interests proved to be invaluable to me. You can't connect the dots looking forward; you can only connect them looking backwards. So, you have to trust that the dots will somehow connect in your future. You have to trust in something - your

gut, destiny, life, karma, whatever. This approach has never let me down, and it has made all the difference in my life.
Steve Jobs

Hmmm "Two roads diverged in woods . . ."

Little decisions can be made quickly and give the big decisions more time. Save your mental bandwidth for the big stuff.

Decide to be an adult. Kids do what feels good and adults do what is good.

Stop Stress Relieving and Begin Goal Achieving

Goals are important because they fix your eyes on a destination. It's like driving, your car goes where your eyes go. It's your attitude that creates an atmosphere that drives action.

This idea is captured perfectly in *The Breviary of Medieval Knights* (a breviary is a book containing the service for each day, to be recited by those in orders):

"This is the Knight's Path. An easy and hard path at the same time, as it urges us to let aside useless things and relative friendships."

"That is why, at the beginning, we hesitate so much to follow it."

"This is a Knight's first teaching: you will erase everything you wrote up to now on your life's notebook: turmoil, insecurities, lies."

"And in place of all that, you will write the word courage."

"Beginning the journey with this word and going on with faith in God, you will arrive where you need to arrive."

The motion for courage in sign language is two hands touching the chest, bringing them forward while forming clenched fists. It's like tapping into your heart, connecting your "why," facing the fear and fighting by standing strong with resolve. I like that.

Apollo astronauts were depressed after returning from landing on the moon. What do you do for an encore? They needed other goals. Without a goal they became depressed. What makes you think you are any different. Have a dream, set a goal.

Not realizing what you want is a problem of knowledge. Not pursuing what you want is a problem of motivation. Not achieving what you want is a problem of persistence.

So, if you don't know, learn and discover. If you're not motivated, maybe it's really not your goal or maybe you need some coaching.

Decide to Find Your "Why"

"Where there is no vision, the people perish." Proverbs 29:18

Decide to take action. Procrastination fuels depression by putting off your desire, while action toward your goal, fuels hope.

"Hope deferred makes the heart sick, but desire fulfilled is a tree of life." Proverbs 13:12

My biggest decision happened after one of my greatest hair-raising experiences while working at Fifth Third Bank in Indianapolis. It was a cold January morning when a man walked into the bank coughing and sneezing from the frigid temperature. He held a handkerchief to his face as he coughed and then pulled a gun on me!

The end of a gun is relatively small but when it is 6" from your face it looks like the end of a canon. He got his money and took me hostage. We left the bank in my car and while he was trying to start the car, I looked right at him. Then he put the gun in my face and said "If you look at me again, I'll shoot you right here, right now. Look out the window!"

I did as I was told.

He let me go, but he still had a hold on me. A flurry of "what if" questions flooded my mind as I lay in bed and tried in vain to sleep.

"What if I died?"

"What if I was a cripple?"

"What if I was brain damaged?"

There were a ton of things I wanted to do, and I wasn't on track to do any of them. What if I died? What then? Was there a God and what did He think about me and how I was living?

I needed to figure some things out!

I went to the library and studied the major world religions. I concluded that only one made sense, only one encouraged logic and reason applied to evidence and only one was true. I decided to place my trust in the *Bible* and God's Son, Jesus Christ. That one decision was the catalyst, the foundation and hope for my future ever since.

As a result of that decision, I got married, we had children. I started meeting with Dr Dave DeWitt. For over 25 years I have been meeting with "doc" every Thursday morning where he introduced me to Turkish blend coffee and helped open the *Bible* to me.

One thing you need to know about "doc" is that he is about as cuddly as a cactus. The other thing you need to know is that he is a *Bible* guy. Not a church guy, not a religion guy, not a spiritual or emotional guy, but a *Bible* guy. I wanted to learn the *Bible* and there is no better *Bible* teacher in the world.

He is like my *Bible* drug dealer. He delivers pure and uncut *Bible* teaching. I like that. If I were a crack addict, I would go to the dealer who had the "good stuff." If it was too potent, I could always cut it at home, but don't sell me impure stuff.

That's how doc serves up the *Bible*. Pure and uncut.

Remember, Being Decisive is Attractive

Develop this idea: culture, media, etc., discourages personal freedom, judging, truth, etc., BUT they are ALL IN when it comes to sexual freedom and expression. Acting on that type of "freedom" is one of the most destructive things you can do to yourself. And by the way, it isn't 'freedom' at all. It's the worst kind of bondage, a karma-biting snake, that strikes again and again until you stop.

Willink, who wakes up at 4:30 a.m., says that anyone has the capacity to become a morning person. Having the discipline to wake up early isn't something that you're "born with," the leadership coach and author tells *Make It*. "You just decide that's what you're going to do. ... You choose to live your life that way."

In the *Entrepreneur* article, "11 Things To Do in Your 20's to be a Millionaire by 30," number 4 on the list is:

Be Disciplined and Decisive

Rafael Badziag, an expert in the psychology of entrepreneurship, discusses the long-term habits of billionaires in his book *"The Billion Dollar Secret: 20 Principles of Billionaire Wealth and Success."*

He spent five years interviewing 21 self-made billionaires and found that along with other things, they are all disciplined, Business Insider previously reported.

"The billionaires I interviewed are the most disciplined people I have ever met," Badziag wrote. "They put a high standard on themselves and on the people around them."

After studying over 500 millionaires, journalist and author Napoleon Hill found that they all shared one quality: decisiveness.

"Analysis of several hundred people who had accumulated fortunes well beyond the million-dollar mark disclosed the fact that every one of them had the habit of reaching decisions promptly," Napoleon Hill wrote in his 1937 personal-finance classic *Think and Grow Rich*.

"In order to make better decisions you must understand that we are all somehow irrational creatures and that our decisions are mostly driven by our emotions." *Never Split the Difference* by Chris Voss

My hope is that you have learned at least one good idea to help you make better decisions in your life.

God bless you,

RJ Regan

About The Author

Robert Regan, or "RJ" as his friends call him, was touted by Post Malone as the "coolest man in Grand Rapids, Michigan" in 2016. He connects with people honestly and openly and is the type of person who just makes you feel

good when you are around him. The attention he gives you is the type that makes you feel as if you were the most important person in the world. He is a "serial entrepreneur" and father of four adult children.

He has earned degrees in Finance from Indiana University as well as an MBA from the DeVos Graduate School of Management at Northwood University. He has professional experience as a banker, stockbroker, operations research manager, business owner, real estate investor, author, speaker, and even politics. His Grey Cap Transportation business takes him all across the country delivering large trucks and experiencing what each state has to offer.

References

Belludi. Nagesh. "Make a Difficult Decision Like Benjamin Franklin." 2015. https://www.rightattitudes.com/2015/10/30/decision-making-benjamin-franklin/.

Carroll, Lewis. Alice in Wonderland. 1866.

Draper, Herbert James. Homer and the Sirens. https://artuk.org/discover/artworks/ulysses-and-the-sirens-78281/view_as/grid/search/keyword:draper--venue:ferens-art-gallery-3518/page/1.

Jackson, Eric. "The Only Thing You Need To Remember About The Seven Habits of Highly Effective People." Forbes. 2012.
https://www.forbes.com/sites/ericjackson/2012/07/24/the-only-thing-you-need-to-remember-about-the-seven-habits-of-highly-effective-people/#202e260467f7.

Kuldip Singh. "An Old Cherokee is Teaching His Grandson About Life." Medium. 2016. https://medium.com/@kuldip_mankul65/an-old-cherokee-is-teaching-his-grandson-about-life-7eee81f09b70.

Wikipedia. Image of Sitting Bull. https://en.wikipedia.org/wiki/Sitting_Bull.